Plantiful

Over 75 Vibrant *Vegan* Comfort Foods

Francesca Bonadonna

VICTORY BELT PUBLISHING INC.

Las Vegas

First published in 2021 by Victory Belt Publishing Inc.

ISBN-13: 978-1-628604-21-4

Cover design by Charisse Reyes and Justin-Aaron Velasco

Interior design and illustrations by Yordan Terziev and Boryana Yordanova

Food photography by Francesca Bonadonna

Lifestyle photography by Peter Valcarcel

Printed in Canada

TC 0121

table of contents

introduction

I have been surrounded my whole life by people who love delicious food. I grew up in an Italian family who knew how to cook like you wouldn't believe, and no one used a recipe or a measuring cup. Techniques were passed down from one generation to the next. I was fortunate to grow up with four grandparents and four great-grandparents, all of whom instilled a passion for cooking and food in me. I've included vegan versions of some of the meals that I enjoyed with them in this book. But of all the amazing meals I have eaten, my mom's will always take the cake. She knows how to turn simple ingredients and spices into the best meal you could imagine. She has had the most influence on how I cook and choose flavors.

Mom was a bit surprised when her mozzarella-loving daughter announced in April 2016 that she wanted to be a vegan. To be honest, my whole family was shocked. How could I be Italian and be a vegan? How was I ever going to resist all of the foods I had grown up eating and enjoying? Surely it was just a phase, and I would be back to eating meatballs in a week. Well, I'll tell you, it was not a phase, and I have figured out how to make a vegan version of every food I have ever loved.

People think vegans have amazing willpower because they don't eat animal products, but I don't think that's the case. I think those of us who decide to go vegan or plant-based have just realized that animal products aren't as essential to making a delicious meal as people believe they are. No matter what you cook, you season it with herbs and spices to make it flavorful. Plants are pretty amazing, and in this book we are going to have a whole lot of fun exploring just how good they can taste.

I am all about comfort food. If a meal doesn't make you feel good and happy when you eat it, then why bother? This book shows you how to make comfort food that is satisfying while still being somewhat healthy. Some of the recipes are a bit more decadent than others, but life is all about enjoying things in moderation.

Whether you are a new vegan or a seasoned vegan, or you are simply interested in trying some plant-based recipes, I promise there is something in here for you. I created everything with love, and I am so excited to share it. My recipes have been enjoyed by non-vegans and vegans alike. While my family and I may eat differently now, they are always eager to try the food I make. My hope is that these become recipes that you share with your family, friends, and loved ones, too.

I want this book to provide you with recipes that defy what you imagine vegan food is and inspire you to try new things. Prior to going vegan, I thought all vegan food was bland and gross. I was finishing up my master's in vocal performance while living in New York City when my eyes were opened. I started to try more vegan restaurants and found that I really enjoyed the food. I gave veganism a shot for thirty days and started a small, private Instagram account to use as a food diary. Then the Instagram started to grow, and suddenly I had a blog and a YouTube channel, and people were re-creating my recipes at home.

Life did a 180 for me, and while I will always love singing, I am so happy to be doing something else that I am passionate about. Sharing these recipes with you in my very own cookbook is truly a dream come true, and I am so thankful for all of the support I have had along the way. I am so excited for you to try these recipes!

a guide to the recipes

Everything in this book is 100 percent vegan, which means that the recipes do not call for any animal products or by-products. So, instead of using an egg, you will use an egg replacer (see pages 11–12); instead of cow's milk, you will use a nondairy milk. Most of the replacements are easy to find in grocery stores or online. I always say that vegan cooking isn't and shouldn't seem hard or scary because you aren't cooking with raw meat or eggs. In my opinion, vegan recipes are actually easier to make than their non-vegan counterparts because there is less to worry about with regard to the possibility of undercooking or overcooking your food.

This cookbook takes you through many ways of preparing meat, egg, and dairy alternatives. The meat alternatives are seitan- or soy-based. The homemade egg alternatives, found primarily in the breakfast chapter, are made from chickpea flour and tofu. The dairy alternatives are nut-, soy-, and vegetable-based. Through the use of various cooking methods such as baking, boiling, pan-frying, sautéing, and steaming, you are going to transform these ingredients into comforting vegan dishes.

You will also be using store-bought ingredients like egg replacer, vegan butter, vegan cheese, vegan cream cheese, and vegan ground beef. These alternatives should be easy to find at bigger grocery chains such as Kroger, Sprouts, Trader Joe's, and Whole Foods. The next section walks you through some of the staple ingredients for vegan cooking.

When shopping for ingredients, please remember to read the packaging labels on foods. Some products have a vegan certification noting that the item is completely vegan-friendly. However, many mainstream brands do not include this certification. Labels that read "processed in a facility with dairy, eggs, milk, etc." are there for allergen purposes; they let you know that these products could have come in contact with these allergens but do not contain them. These are fine to eat and to use in vegan cooking. However, if a label says, "may contain trace amounts of dairy/eggs/milk/etc.," the item likely contains that allergen. I tend to steer clear of those products just to be safe.

Vegan baking tends to work just like regular baking. In fact, plant-based alternatives like vegan butter work at a 1:1 ratio to their non-vegan counterparts, so I find that vegan baking is sometimes even easier than vegan cooking. Most of the methods used in these recipes mirror the traditional preparation methods, with the exception of the Cream Puffs (page 166), which do not contain eggs, the main leavening agent in traditional cream puffs.

The recipes in this book call for the vegetables and seasonings that I have found to produce the best results. However, if you can't find a certain ingredient or you need to make a swap, it will probably be okay. For example, if you don't have Vidalia onions (my favorite!), you can use another type of sweet onion; if you want to change the Spinach Quiche (page 34) to a broccoli quiche, it will still taste great. If you don't have a particular herb or spice on hand, it is fine to swap it for something similar or omit it altogether. Be sure to give your meals a taste before serving and adjust any seasonings or spices to your preferences.

The recipes are grouped by type—breakfasts, main dishes, desserts, and so on—with the addition of the Bites and Comfort Bowls chapters, which feature some of my favorite snacks and meals-in-a-bowl. Each chapter is focused on comfort food and features recipes from a variety of cuisines.

If you are a vegan, I hope I can teach you something new or give you a new favorite recipe. If this is your first time cooking a plant-based meal, get ready to have some fun. Don't be scared, and trust me when I say that you won't mess anything up. A recipe made with love will always taste delicious!

ingredient guide

This section covers staple ingredients such as salt, sugar, and pasta, as well as some lesser-known ingredients and where to find them. If you come across an ingredient in a recipe that is confusing to you, I have likely covered it here.

ALMOND PASTE: A product made from ground almonds, sugar, and water. While the ingredients are similar to those used in marzipan, almond paste is a different product. It has a stronger flavor and is not as smooth as marzipan, which makes it great for baking; you'll see it used in my Rainbow Cookies (page 172).

CASHEWS: A type of tree nut that can be soaked in water and used in recipes to create a creamy texture. When using cashews for this purpose, it is important to either soak them in the refrigerator overnight or boil them for 30 minutes prior to use. This softens them and helps them break down more thoroughly when blended. After cashews are soaked or boiled, they need to drained and rinsed. *Note:* If you have a high-powered blender, such as a Vitamix or Blendtec, you can use either the overnight soak or the quicker 30-minute boil to soften them. However, if you are using a regular blender, I recommend that you soak the cashews overnight for the best results.

COCONUT MILK: A canned coconut-based product. There are several varieties— some are full-fat and others are light. I typically use light and have found it to be just as creamy, but full-fat is fine, too. You'll see coconut milk used in my Thai Red Curry Roasted Cauliflower Bowl (page 98) and my Yellow Split Pea Cannellini Bean Stew (page 120). I do not recommend using boxed and refrigerated coconut milk in these recipes.

COCOWHIP: A coconut-based alternative to whipped topping (such as Cool Whip) made by the company So Delicious. Like Cool Whip, Cocowhip comes frozen and can be used straight from the freezer or thawed, if desired (it needs to thaw for only 1 to 2 minutes before use). It is great for topping baked goods and pies. I suggest using this product over homemade coconut whipped cream, which can be unreliable. However, if you have a reliable recipe for homemade coconut whipped cream that you like, feel free to use it.

EGG REPLACER: A product that is usually made from potato starch. You mix it with water and use it to replace eggs in baked goods. Follow the package directions for the brand you purchase. Popular brands include Bob's Red Mill, Ener-G Egg Replacer, and The Neat Egg.

A homemade alternative is a flax or chia egg. To make one, you mix 1 tablespoon of flaxseed meal or chia seeds with 1 tablespoon of water, set it aside until it thickens, and then use it in your recipe as you would an egg. However, I prefer the store-bought egg replacer products because they blend in more seamlessly, and I tend to have better success with them.

GOCHUJANG PASTE: A spicy Korean chili paste. It's a key ingredient in my Sweet Gochujang Tempeh Bao (page 70). It can be found at many grocery stores, in Asian markets, and online.

NONDAIRY MILK: A dairy-free milk alternative that can be made from nuts, seeds, or grains. Unless otherwise noted, be sure to use an unflavored and unsweetened nondairy milk for the recipes in this book. Otherwise, you may end up altering the flavor of the dish, possibly in an unpleasant way. This is especially important when cooking savory dishes. When a recipe calls for nondairy milk, any nondairy milk you like will work; however, do not use canned coconut milk. Canned coconut milk (see page 11) is thicker than boxed and refrigerated nondairy milks and doesn't work exactly the same in recipes.

NUTRITIONAL YEAST: An inactive yeast that comes in large flakes. Unlike active dry yeast, nutritional yeast is a food product. It has a yellow color and a savory cheesy flavor, making it perfect for adding cheesiness to a dish. Note that nutritional yeast provides the flavor but not the texture of cheese; to replicate that texture, you will need to add other ingredients, like cashews, potatoes, or tofu. Nutritional yeast is used in recipes like the Vegan Mac and Cheese (page 132) and Tofu Ricotta (page 188).

PASTA: Various types of dried pasta are used throughout this book. Dried pasta is typically vegan-friendly, while fresh pasta usually contains egg. It is important to check the box just in case. My favorite type of pasta is 100 percent durum semolina; however, feel free to use whatever is accessible to you.

Different types and sizes of pasta require different amounts of time to cook, so it's best to follow the cooking instructions given on the box of pasta you're cooking (note that the cooking time will either be given as a specific amount of time or in a range of minutes). The cooking time on the box is generally for cooking pasta until it is al dente, which means "to the tooth." Pasta cooked al dente is just cooked through and retains a pleasant firmness or resistance at the center when you bite into it. This typically takes 8 to 12 minutes, depending on the pasta. Al dente is considered the perfect way to cook pasta; however, we all have our own pasta doneness preferences. When I refer to pasta being slightly undercooked, you should cook it 1 to 2 minutes less than the cooking time stated on the box because it will finish cooking in a final step (usually in the oven, as when making lasagna). Finally, when I refer to pasta being cooked 1 to 2 minutes past al dente, it should be cooked until it is a bit softer than al dente, but not to the point of being mushy. To test the doneness of pasta, scoop a piece out of the cooking water and try it 2 minutes before the suggested cooking time has elapsed and again at the end of the suggested cooking time. From there, you can adjust the cooking time to your pasta doneness preference.

When cooking pasta that will be mixed with a sauce, I recommend that you reserve ½ cup (120ml) of the starchy cooking water. After the pasta is done, carefully reserve the pasta water and set it aside. It will thin the sauce a bit without making it as thin as plain water would.

SALT: An essential flavor enhancer. The main salt used in all of the recipes in this book is regular fine-grain table salt. Different types and grinds of salt are more or less salty than others, so be prepared to adjust the amounts if you use another type. I also use coarse sea salt in some recipes, but usually only as a garnish.

SOY CURLS: A soy-based alternative to meat made from non-GMO soybeans; they have a texture similar to chicken. Soy curls are sold dehydrated, so they need to be rehydrated before use. They are very versatile and can be added to soups or stir-fries or served on their own tossed in a sauce; in this book, they are used in my Chick'n and Dumplings recipe (page 148). Soy curls are made by Butler Foods and can be purchased online; some larger grocery stores carry them, too.

SUGAR: The classic sweetener. In this book, I use granulated sugar, dark brown sugar, and confectioners' (aka powdered) sugar. I specify organic for all three types because some sugars are processed with bone char, making them unfriendly to vegans. Organic sugar is bone char–free and can be found at most grocery stores. There are two options for organic sugar: cane sugar and beet sugar. I prefer organic cane sugar because it tends to be easier to source, and I find it to be more similar to white sugar. You can use either type, depending on your preference.

TAPIOCA STARCH (aka tapioca flour): An important ingredient for making vegan cheese, such as my Homemade Vegan Mozzarella (page 190). You must cook tapioca starch to activate it; when activated, it develops a gooey cheeselike texture. You can find it at most grocery stores and online. Bob's Red Mill is the most popular brand.

TEMPEH: A soy-based product made from fermented soybeans. Tempeh has a strong and slightly bitter flavor, so it's important to boil or steam it to take away the bitterness before use. Tempeh is less processed than tofu (see page 14); some people prefer it for this reason. The fact that tempeh is fermented also makes it beneficial for gut health. Due to its naturally rough texture, it works well to give dishes like my Meaty Vegan Burgers (page 118) a meaty feel.

TEXTURED VEGETABLE PROTEIN (TVP): A soy-based product made from defatted soy flour. It comes dried and needs to be rehydrated before use. Its texture makes it a handy replacement for ground meat, as in Betty Grandma's Meatballs (page 52). Bob's Red Mill is the most popular brand. Sometimes you'll find it labeled as textured soy protein (TSP); it is the same product.

TOFU: A soy-based product that typically comes in block form. Tofu is typically found in the produce section of the grocery store. There are several different firmnesses, most of which are packaged in a container of water. Silken/soft tofu is very soft and great for sauces and desserts, like "cheesecake" (see page 170). Medium firm/firm tofu is good for a tofu scramble or for making Tofu Ricotta (page 188). Extra-firm tofu is very firm and works well in stir-fries; you'll see it used in a couple of my comfort bowl recipes. Super-firm (high-protein) tofu comes in no water and is vacuum sealed. It is the firmest tofu and is good for stir-fries, pan-frying, or deep-frying; I use it in my Popcorn Chick'n (page 62). Leftover tofu can be stored in a container with water for up to 5 days; be sure to change the water daily.

Some people press their firm or extra-firm tofu prior to use, but I typically don't. Pressing helps the tofu hold its shape a bit better once you cut it; however, this tends to be less of a problem with extra-firm tofu. If you would like to press your tofu, you can purchase a tofu press online or simply wrap the tofu in a paper towel, place it a pan, put a few cans on top, and let it sit for 5 to 10 minutes. Do not attempt to press silken/soft tofu.

VEGAN BUTTER: An alternative to dairy butter that is typically made from whipped oils. Some brands use nuts as a base, so pay attention to the ingredients if you have a nut sensitivity or allergy. Vegan butter typically comes salted. Like regular butter, it may need to be softened or melted prior to use in a recipe. When a recipe calls for cold vegan butter, it should be used straight from the refrigerator. Popular brands include Earth Balance, I Can't Believe It's Not Butter, and Miyoko's Cultured Vegan Butter.

VEGAN CHEDDAR/MOZZARELLA SHREDS: A shredded cheese alternative that is typically made from various starches, oils, and flavorings. Most brands are soy- and nut-free. Popular brands include Daiya, Follow Your Heart, Violife, and Whole Foods 365. Note that this book includes a recipe for Homemade Vegan Mozzarella (page 190); however, this cheese alternative has the texture of a thick molten cheese sauce and will not shred.

VEGAN CHORIZO: A soy-based alternative to chorizo, a highly seasoned pork sausage that's often used in Mexican and Spanish dishes. Similar to chorizo, vegan chorizo is salty, savory, and spicy. It must be removed from its plastic casing and crumbled before use. Trader Joe's Soy Chorizo is a popular store brand, and others can be found online.

VEGAN CREAM CHEESE: A cream cheese alternative that is typically made from nuts or soy. Popular brands include Daiya, Follow Your Heart, Kite Hill, and Tofutti. It is used in many sweet and savory dishes in this book, from the Mini Salted Caramel "Cheesecake" (page 170) to the Vegan Mac and Cheese (page 132).

VEGAN FOOD DYES: Not all food dyes are vegan-friendly due to the ingredients used in the artificial colors. You'll need red and green dyes to make my Rainbow Cookies (page 172). Popular brands include Chefmaster and India Tree.

VEGAN GROUND BEEF: A meat alternative that is used to replace ground beef, as in my Meaty Vegan Lasagna (page 110). It is typically soy- or pea protein–based; however, food companies are always experimenting with new ingredients. Popular brands include Beyond Meat, Gardein, Impossible Foods, LightLife, and Trader Joe's Beef-less Ground Beef.

VEGAN PARMESAN: A Parmesan cheese alternative that is typically made from oils and various flavorings. Popular brands include Follow Your Heart and Go Veggie.

VEGAN SOUR CREAM: A sour cream alternative that can be coconut-, nut-, or soy-based. It is available at most grocery stores. Popular brands include Follow Your Heart and Tofutti. In this book, I use vegan sour cream to add richness to both savory and sweet recipes.

VEGAN SPRINKLES: Most sprinkles are not vegan-friendly due to the confectioner's glaze they contain, which is derived from insects. There are many vegan sprinkle options available online, and that is the best place to purchase them.

VEGAN WHIPPED CREAM: A canned almond- or coconut-based alternative to store-bought dairy-based whipped cream. (This is different from Cocowhip, which replaces whipped topping, not whipped cream; see page 11.) It is used in the Cream Puffs recipe (page 166). I prefer using canned vegan whipped cream to making homemade coconut whipped cream for my recipes. I find the store-bought whipped cream to be more reliable due to the added stabilizers; it is also lighter and airier than homemade coconut whipped cream. Reddi-wip and Trader Joe's are popular brands.

VITAL WHEAT GLUTEN: The main protein in wheat. It is the primary ingredient in seitan, which replaces chicken in my Buffalo Chick'n Sandwiches (page 108) and Chick'n Marsala (page 126). Vital wheat gluten helps give seitan its stretchy, meatlike texture. It can also be used to replace beef. It can be purchased at most grocery stores and online. Bob's Red Mill is the most popular brand.

1.

breakfast comfort

A vegan breakfast may seem like a bit of an obstacle. When I first went vegan, I thought my only options were oatmeal and avocado toast. In this chapter, however, you will find ten amazing vegan breakfasts, both savory and sweet, ranging from Homemade Croissants to a Vegan Omelette. There are options for quick and easy weekday breakfasts as well as more time-consuming dishes that are great for a leisurely brunch.

In this chapter, we will explore ways to substitute for eggs by using chickpea flour and tofu. You are also going to get the best vegan "buttermilk" pancake recipe you could ask for—I promise fluffy pancakes every time. Grab some fruit and a cup of tea or coffee, and let's start the day off right!

vegan chorizo and potato breakfast tacos

Yield: 8 tacos (4 servings)

Prep Time: 15 minutes, plus time to pickle onions

Cook Time: 35 minutes

Try something different with these fun breakfast tacos. They have a lot of flavorful elements that work wonderfully together. The quick pickled onions add some sweetness and tang, the vegan chorizo and potatoes are savory and filling, and the refried beans help hold everything together. The pickled onions can be made ahead and will keep in the fridge for up to 5 days. Be sure to check the ingredients in your refried beans and tortillas, as they sometimes include lard.

QUICK PICKLED ONIONS

1 red onion (about 8 ounces/225g), thinly sliced

¼ cup (60ml) apple cider vinegar

1 tablespoon maple syrup

1 teaspoon salt

FILLING

4 large Yukon Gold potatoes (about 1½ pounds/680g), cut into ¾-inch (2cm) chunks

¼ onion, preferably Vidalia (about 2 ounces/55g), chopped

2 tablespoons olive oil, divided

½ teaspoon chili powder

½ teaspoon garlic powder

½ teaspoon paprika

¼ teaspoon salt

8 ounces (225g) vegan chorizo

1 (15-ounce/425g) can vegan refried beans

8 medium tortillas (about 8 inches/20cm)

4 sprigs fresh cilantro, for garnish

1 lime, cut into wedges, for serving

1. Prepare the pickled onions: Place all of the ingredients along with 1 cup (240ml) of water in a large jar and leave on the counter for at least 30 minutes. This can be done ahead of time and left in the refrigerator overnight.

2. Preheat the oven to 425°F (218°C). Line a rimmed baking sheet with parchment paper.

3. Prepare the filling: In a large bowl, mix together the potatoes, onion, 1½ tablespoons of the olive oil, and the seasonings. Spread out on the prepared baking sheet and bake for 25 minutes, until golden and crispy.

4. Meanwhile, remove the vegan chorizo from the casing. Sauté the chorizo with the remaining ½ tablespoon of oil in a medium-sized nonstick frying pan over medium heat for 5 to 7 minutes, until crispy.

5. Heat up the refried beans either in the microwave for 1 minute or in a small saucepan on the stovetop over medium heat for 5 minutes.

6. When the potatoes and onion are done, mix them with the chorizo.

7. Wrap the tortillas in a damp paper towel and microwave for 1 minute, or warm them in a large nonstick frying pan for 2 to 3 minutes.

8. To assemble the tacos, spread 2 to 3 tablespoons of the refried beans on a tortilla. Top with one-eighth of the filling, then with a few pickled onions. Repeat until all of the tacos are made. Garnish with the cilantro and serve with lime wedges.

quick breakfast sandwich

Yield: 1 sandwich

Prep Time: 5 minutes

Cook Time: 12 minutes

I have eaten this sandwich almost every day for a year. It is my absolute favorite breakfast. If you miss egg sandwiches, you must try this recipe, which uses chickpea flour to create egglike patties. Use any bread and vegan meat replacement you like. This recipe is very easy to customize, so you can use whatever you have on hand! Serve the sandwich with your favorite fruit.

CHICKPEA PATTIES

¼ cup (30g) chickpea flour

1½ teaspoons nutritional yeast

Pinch of turmeric powder

Pinch of salt

Pinch of ground black pepper

1 vegan English muffin

2 slices vegan turkey

1 slice vegan cheddar cheese

1. Prepare the chickpea patties: In a medium-sized bowl, whisk together all of the ingredients. Pour in ¼ cup (60ml) of water and whisk again until smooth.

2. Lightly coat a medium-sized nonstick frying pan with cooking spray. Pour in the batter in 2 equal-sized circles. Cook over medium-low heat for 5 minutes, or until the edges and tops of the patties start to look dry. Use a spatula to flip and cook for 5 minutes on the other side. If you cannot easily move the chickpea patties with the spatula to flip them, they need more time to cook.

3. Cut the English muffin in half and place both halves cut side down in the pan for 1 minute to warm them. Remove from the pan.

4. Assemble the sandwich: Place the vegan turkey slices on the bottom half of the English muffin, then the chickpea patties. Place the vegan cheese and the top bun on top of the patties. Place the sandwich in the pan and pour in 1 tablespoon of water. Cover with a lid and cook for 30 seconds to 1 minute, until the vegan cheese is melted. Enjoy warm.

"eggs" in purgatory

Yield: 4 to 6 servings
Prep Time: 10 minutes
Cook Time: 35 minutes

Move over, shakshuka, because "eggs" in purgatory are here to stay. This southern Italian dish is spicy and fiery, which pairs nicely with the creaminess of the tofu. Eggs in purgatory is traditionally served with eggs, but tofu makes a great replacement. The tofu is cooked right on top of the sauce, and this meal is best eaten hot out of the pan with a lot of crusty bread. This is a great recipe for brunch with friends or family; feel free to tone down the spiciness if it is too much for you.

1 tablespoon olive oil

2 cloves garlic, minced

⅛ onion, preferably Vidalia (about 1 ounce/28g), chopped

Coarse sea salt

Red pepper flakes

1 (28-ounce/794g) can crushed fire-roasted tomatoes

1 tablespoon organic granulated sugar

1 teaspoon paprika

15 grape tomatoes, halved

12 ounces (340g) firm tofu

1 teaspoon nutritional yeast

½ teaspoon garlic powder

¼ teaspoon fine salt

Pinch of turmeric powder

3 fresh basil leaves, chiffonaded

1½ teaspoons extra-virgin olive oil, for drizzling

1. Pour the olive oil into a large cast-iron skillet or heavy frying pan over medium-low heat. Add the garlic, onion, and a pinch each of coarse salt and red pepper flakes and cook over medium-low heat, stirring often, for 5 minutes, or until the onion is translucent and the garlic is fragrant.

2. Add the crushed tomatoes, sugar, and paprika to the pan. Mix with a rubber spatula or wooden spoon, then place the grape tomatoes on top of the sauce. Increase the heat to medium, then cover and simmer for 15 to 20 minutes, until the sauce has thickened.

3. Meanwhile, in a medium-sized bowl, crumble the tofu into small pieces using your hands. Sprinkle the nutritional yeast, garlic powder, fine salt, and turmeric over the tofu and mix to combine.

4. Remove the lid from the sauce and arrange the tofu in 6 circles spread across the pan. Cover and cook for 10 minutes, or until the tofu starts to turn yellow.

5. Sprinkle with the basil, a scant teaspoon of red pepper flakes, and a pinch of coarse salt and drizzle with the extra-virgin olive oil.

homemade croissants

Yield: 8 croissants

Prep Time: 45 minutes, plus time to refrigerate

Cook Time: 25 minutes

This recipe might seem daunting because it takes three days to make, but these croissants are so worth it. Most of the time you are just rolling and folding the dough and then placing it back in the refrigerator, so don't be intimidated. I did learn along the way that the more you practice, the better they come out each time, so don't give up if your first try isn't perfect. Also, be sure to have a measuring tape because it comes in handy!

DOUGH

1 (¼-ounce/7g) packet active dry yeast

2½ tablespoons (30g) organic granulated sugar, divided

3 cups (360g) all-purpose flour, plus more for dusting

2 tablespoons vegan butter, melted

VEGAN BUTTER LAYER

¾ cup (168g) cold vegan butter, sliced

2 tablespoons nondairy milk, for brushing

DAY 1

1.   Prepare the dough: Pour the yeast into ¾ cup (180ml) of warm water that is between 100°F and 110°F (37°C and 43°C). Add ½ tablespoon of the sugar and set aside to proof for 10 minutes, until foamy.

2.   Meanwhile, in a large bowl, whisk the flour and the remaining 2 tablespoons of sugar. Pour in the melted vegan butter and activated yeast. Mix with a rubber spatula until a shaggy dough forms. Knead the dough by hand for 5 minutes, until it is smooth.

3.   Place the dough in a 9-inch (23cm) pie pan and lightly dust the top with flour. Cover with plastic wrap and refrigerate for at least 8 hours or overnight.

4.   Prepare the vegan butter layer: On a large piece of parchment paper, trace a 7-inch (18cm) square. Flip the parchment over so you can see the square but you are not rolling the butter on the side with writing. Lay the slices of vegan butter around the perimeter and inside of the square, then top with another piece of parchment paper. Using a rolling pin, roll the butter inward to the center and then back out to the corners until you have a solid square that is the size of the traced square, making sure the thickness is uniform. Fold the parchment paper over the butter and refrigerate for 8 hours or overnight.

DAY 2

5.   Remove the dough from the refrigerator. It will have become a bit bigger, but will not have doubled in size. On a clean, lightly floured surface, roll out the dough into an 11-inch (28cm) square.

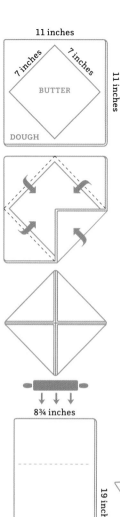

6. Remove the butter layer from the parchment and place it on top of the dough square on a diagonal, so the butter looks like a diamond shape. Fold the corners of the dough over the butter so that all of the butter is covered and it forms a square.

7. Using a rolling pin and even pressure, lightly tap up and down the dough to flatten and disperse the butter. Then carefully and gently roll the dough into an 8¾ by 19-inch (22 by 48cm) rectangle. Rolling the dough with even pressure is important to ensure the butter layer is evenly dispersed.

8. Make the first series of folds: With a short end of the rectangle facing you, bring the bottom of the rectangle three-quarters of the way up over the dough. Then bring the top (the edge farthest from you) a quarter of the way down to meet the edge of the folded dough. The dough will now be a square. Finally, fold the bottom part, closest to you, over the top part to make a rectangle about 4½ by 8¾ inches (11.5 by 22cm). When you look at it from the side, you will see three thick layers of dough. Gently tap the dough with the rolling pin to slightly flatten the butter (you don't want to completely squish the butter layer into the dough). Cover with plastic wrap and refrigerate for 1 hour.

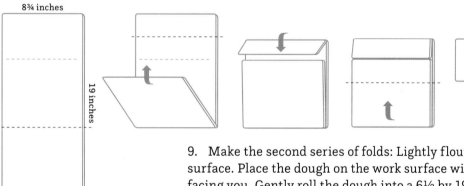

9. Make the second series of folds: Lightly flour a clean work surface. Place the dough on the work surface with a short end facing you. Gently roll the dough into a 6½ by 19-inch (17 by 48cm) rectangle. Bring the top edge, farthest from you, a third of the way down, then bring the bottom edge, closest to you, over the folded dough to form a square.

10. Cover the dough with plastic wrap and refrigerate for 8 hours or overnight.

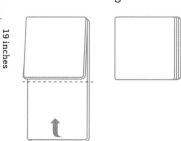

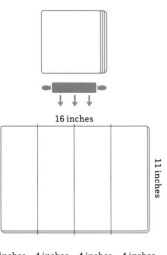

16 inches

11 inches

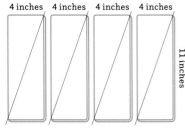

4 inches 4 inches 4 inches 4 inches

11 inches

DAY 3

11. Line a rimmed baking sheet with parchment paper. On a clean, lightly floured surface, roll out the dough into a 16 by 11-inch (40 by 28cm) rectangle, with a long edge facing you.

12. Along the bottom and top edges, mark off four 4-inch (10cm) rectangles. Use a sharp knife to cut the rectangles. Then carefully cut each rectangle in half on a diagonal to make 2 triangles, resulting in 8 triangles.

13. Lightly roll a triangle to elongate it. Cut a small slit, about ¼ inch (6mm) long, at the top of the triangle, then gently pull it apart to stretch the opening. Then roll the triangle from the top part with the slit down to the point. Tuck the tip of the triangle under the croissant and place the croissant on the prepared baking sheet. Repeat until all 8 croissants have been made.

14. Cover the croissants with a clean kitchen towel and proof them at room temperature, away from drafts (inside the oven with the oven light on is an ideal spot), for 1 to 2 hours, until they have almost doubled in size. When proofed, they should jiggle slightly when you shake the pan.

15. Before baking, refrigerate the croissants for at least 1 hour but no longer than 8 hours. Chilling the croissants helps keep the vegan butter cold so it will not melt everywhere as the croissants bake.

16. When ready to bake the croissants, preheat the oven to 400°F (204°C).

17. Bake the croissants for 10 minutes. Lower the heat to 375°F (190°C) and bake for another 8 minutes. Rotate the pan 180 degrees, then bake for 7 minutes more, or until the croissants are golden brown and crispy. Enjoy them warm out of the oven.

The best vegan butter for this recipe is the stick form; however, if you cannot find that, you can use one packaged in a tub. The most accurate way to measure the butter for this recipe, whether in stick form or from a tub, is with a kitchen scale. Otherwise, you can use the volume measurement. (If using butter in a tub, use a ¼-cup/60ml measuring cup to scoop out ¾ cup/168g and drop it by the tablespoon around the perimeter of the square when preparing the butter layer on day 1.)

Leftover croissants will keep for 1 to 2 days in a sealed container. To reheat, microwave for 30 seconds or place in a preheated 350°F (176°C) oven for 2 to 3 minutes or until warm.

vegan buttermilk pancakes

Yield: 8 large or 16 small pancakes (4 servings)

Prep Time: 7 minutes

Cook Time: 40 minutes

Everyone should know how to make fluffy pancakes. This vegan version requires only a few ingredients that you probably already have on hand, and they will put a smile on everyone's face. Add as many toppings as you like, such as maple syrup and fresh blueberries, raspberries, or strawberries. If you have leftovers, they will keep in the refrigerator for up to 2 days or can be frozen. If refrigerated, you can reheat them in the microwave or in a pan; if frozen, reheat them in a toaster.

2½ cups (600ml) nondairy milk

1½ teaspoons apple cider vinegar

3 cups (360g) all-purpose flour

¼ cup (48g) organic granulated sugar

2 tablespoons baking powder

Pinch of salt

2 tablespoons vanilla extract

1. In a medium-sized bowl, mix together the nondairy milk and vinegar. Set aside to curdle for 3 to 5 minutes.

2. Sift the flour, sugar, baking powder, and salt into a large bowl.

3. Pour the curdled nondairy milk and the vanilla extract into the bowl with the dry ingredients. Mix together to form a slightly lumpy batter; leaving a few lumps makes better pancakes.

4. Lightly grease a large nonstick frying pan with cooking spray and set over medium heat. When the pan is hot, pour in ½ cup (120ml) of the batter. (If you prefer small pancakes, you can use ¼ cup/60ml of batter.) If your pan is big enough, you can cook 2 pancakes a time. Cook the pancake(s) for 3 to 4 minutes, until bubbles have formed on the top.

5. Flip the pancake(s) with a metal spatula and cook for another 2 to 3 minutes, until golden on the second side. Repeat with the remaining batter, adding more cooking spray to the pan as needed, making a total of 8 large or 16 small pancakes.

6. Serve warm, topped as desired.

peanut butter and banana overnight oats

Yield: 2 servings

Prep Time: 10 minutes, plus time to chill

While I've never been a big fan of traditional oatmeal, I love overnight oats, which are thicker and chewier. Paired with the classic combination of peanut butter and banana, these taste like dessert for breakfast. Overnight oats are great for meal prep as well. Just take out a jar when you are ready to eat and top it with extra bananas and peanut butter.

2 bananas (about 8 ounces/225g)

1 cup (90g) rolled oats

⅔ cup (160ml) nondairy milk

3 tablespoons maple syrup

2 tablespoons all-natural peanut butter

2 tablespoons flaxseed meal

FOR TOPPING

½ banana (about 2 ounces/55g) sliced, divided

1 tablespoon all-natural peanut butter, divided

1. In a large bowl, mash the whole bananas with a fork until smooth.

2. Divide the bananas, oats, nondairy milk, maple syrup, peanut butter, and flaxseed meal evenly between two jars. Secure the lids and shake for 1 minute, until everything is mixed together.

3. Refrigerate overnight or for at least 8 hours. The oats should be thick and the liquid absorbed.

4. When ready to eat, top the oat mixture with the sliced banana and peanut butter.

potatoes and "eggs"

Yield: 4 servings

Prep Time: 10 minutes

Cook Time: 45 minutes

Whenever I slept over at my grandma's house—I call her Zucchi—she always cooked me this dish for breakfast. Her version was made with eggs, but here, tofu is used as a replacement, and the result is just as enjoyable. This is a perfect breakfast to serve to family or friends; there is just something special about it being served in a skillet. Top it with ketchup or hot sauce for a delicious breakfast.

2 russet potatoes (about 1½ pounds/680g), chopped

¼ onion, preferably Vidalia (about 2 ounces/55g), chopped

1 tablespoon olive oil

Leaves from 3 to 5 sprigs fresh thyme, or 1 tablespoon dried thyme leaves

1 teaspoon paprika

¼ teaspoon fine salt

¼ teaspoon ground black pepper

TOFU SCRAMBLE

1 (16-ounce/454g) block extra-firm tofu

½ cup (120ml) nondairy milk

1 tablespoon nutritional yeast

¼ teaspoon fine salt

¼ teaspoon ground black pepper

¼ teaspoon turmeric powder

FOR GARNISH

2 tablespoons microgreens

2 sprigs fresh thyme, roughly chopped, or 1 scant teaspoon dried thyme leaves

Pinch of coarse sea salt

Pinch of ground black pepper

1. Place the potatoes in a medium-sized saucepan and cover with water. Boil over high heat until they are softened but not fully cooked, about 15 minutes. Parboiling the potatoes will help them cook quicker in the pan. Once softened, drain the potatoes.

2. When the potatoes have 5 minutes to go, cook the onion in the oil in a large cast-iron skillet or other oven-safe frying pan over low heat for 5 minutes, stirring often. Add the potatoes and seasonings, increase the heat to medium-high, and sauté for 20 minutes, until the potatoes are crispy and golden.

3. Prepare the tofu scramble: In a medium-sized bowl, crumble the tofu into small pieces using your hands. Add the nondairy milk, nutritional yeast, and seasonings and mix together.

4. Add the tofu mixture to the skillet with the potatoes and cook over medium-high heat for 5 minutes, until the tofu starts to turn a vibrant, bright yellow color and the liquid is cooked off. Stir frequently so the tofu becomes well incorporated with the potatoes.

5. Turn the oven broiler to high.

6. Place the skillet in the oven and broil for 5 minutes to crisp the top.

7. Garnish with microgreens, thyme, coarse salt, and pepper and serve.

spinach quiche

Yield: 4 to 6 servings

Prep Time: 25 minutes, plus time to chill dough

Cook Time: 1 hour

Quiche is a breakfast classic. It is easy to make and great for family meals or brunches with friends. Here, silken tofu, chickpea flour, and baking powder work together to create a texture similar to a traditional egg-based quiche. Made with an easy homemade crust and filled with vegetables, this is sure to become a staple in your house. The best part: you can customize it by incorporating different vegetables and vegan cheeses if you like.

CRUST

1½ cups (180g) all-purpose flour, plus more for dusting

1 tablespoon organic granulated sugar

¼ teaspoon fine salt

½ cup (112g) cold vegan butter

FILLING

5 ounces (140g) fresh spinach, chopped

¼ onion, preferably Vidalia (about 2 ounces/55g), chopped

1½ teaspoons olive oil

1 (16-ounce/454g) block silken tofu

1 cup (120g) chickpea flour

¼ cup (60ml) nondairy milk

1 tablespoon nutritional yeast

1 teaspoon garlic powder

1 teaspoon onion powder

¼ teaspoon baking powder

¼ teaspoon fine salt

¼ teaspoon ground black pepper

¼ teaspoon turmeric powder

¼ cup (28g) vegan mozzarella shreds

FOR GARNISH

Coarse sea salt

3 tablespoons microgreens

3 tablespoons sprouts

1. Prepare the crust: In a large bowl, whisk together the flour, sugar, and salt. Cut the vegan butter into the flour using a fork or pastry cutter until small, crumbly pieces have formed. Slowly pour in 3 tablespoons of cold water and continue to mix. The dough will start to become shaggy. Knead with your hands for 3 to 5 minutes, until you can form the dough into a smooth ball. Place in the refrigerator to chill for 30 minutes.

2. Meanwhile, make the filling: In a medium-sized frying pan, sauté the spinach and onion in the oil over medium heat for 5 minutes, until the spinach wilts and the onion is translucent.

3. Place the remaining ingredients for the filling in a blender and blend on high speed until smooth. The mixture should have the thickness of pancake batter.

4. Preheat the oven to 350°F (176°C).

5. Remove the dough from the refrigerator. On a lightly floured surface, roll out the dough to a 10-inch (25cm) circle. Roll the dough over the rolling pin and drape it over a 9-inch (22cm) pie pan. Flute the edges by pinching the dough around the rim of the pan.

6. Spread half of the spinach and onion mixture over the crust. Pour the filling from the blender into the pan. Top with the rest of the spinach and onion mixture, then the vegan mozzarella.

7. Bake for 50 to 55 minutes, until the crust turns golden and the quiche looks somewhat dry on top. If the edge of the crust starts to burn, cover it with aluminum foil.

8. When the quiche is done, let it cool for 5 minutes before slicing. Cut the quiche into 8 pieces, sprinkle with coarse salt, black pepper, and the microgreens and sprouts, and serve.

coffee crumb muffins

Yield: 12 muffins

Prep Time: 15 minutes, plus time to cool

Cook Time: 20 minutes

Muffins are great for a quick and easy breakfast on the go or a fun brunch. I love these coffee crumb muffins because they are less indulgent than coffee cake but still give you that little bit of sweetness. I prefer my muffins not to be overly sweet, so these are only mildly sweet. If you like a sweeter muffin, feel free to increase the amount of sugar (see note below). These are the perfect addition to any breakfast table and will be sure to make just about anyone drool!

MUFFINS

2½ cups (300g) all-purpose flour

⅓ cup (64g) organic dark brown sugar

¼ cup (48g) organic cane sugar

2 teaspoons baking powder

2 teaspoons ground cinnamon

1¼ cups (300ml) nondairy milk

2 tablespoons vegan butter, melted

2 egg replacers (see pages 11–12)

1 teaspoon vanilla extract

CRUMB TOPPING

⅓ cup plus 1 tablespoon (50g) all-purpose flour

½ cup (96g) organic dark brown sugar

¼ cup (44g) vegan butter

2 tablespoons confectioners' sugar, for dusting

1. Preheat the oven to 375°F (190°C). Place 12 paper liners in a standard-size muffin pan.

2. Prepare the muffin batter: Put the dry ingredients in a large bowl and whisk to combine. Add the wet ingredients and mix until a lumpy batter has formed.

3. Pour the batter into the prepared muffin pan, dividing it evenly among the 12 wells. Fill each well about three-quarters of the way full.

4. Rinse and dry the bowl, then prepare the crumb topping in the same bowl. Place all of the topping ingredients in the bowl. Using the back of a fork, mash the vegan butter into the flour and brown sugar until small pea-sized crumbles have formed. Divide the crumb topping evenly among the muffins.

5. Bake the muffins for 20 minutes, or until they are golden and a toothpick comes out clean when inserted into a muffin.

6. Let the muffins cool on a wire rack for 30 minutes before eating. Sift the confectioners' sugar over the muffins and enjoy warm.

If you prefer a sweeter muffin, use ⅔ cup (128g) organic dark brown sugar and ⅓ cup (64g) organic cane sugar.

vegan omelette

Yield: 1 serving
Prep Time: 10 minutes
Cook Time: 25 minutes

A vegan omelette may seem like a contradiction, but trust me when I say that this is one of my favorite breakfasts. Chickpea flour, nondairy yogurt, and coconut milk come together to form an egglike mixture that is a little bit crispy on the outside while being soft and fluffy on the inside. It is important to use an unsweetened and unflavored nondairy yogurt for this recipe.

FILLING

1 teaspoon olive oil

¼ onion (about 2 ounces/55g), chopped

1 cup (85g) frozen broccoli

Pinch of fine salt

Pinch of ground black pepper

¼ cup (28g) vegan cheese shreds of choice

OMELETTE

¼ cup (30g) chickpea flour

2 tablespoons plain nondairy yogurt

½ cup (120ml) canned coconut milk

¼ teaspoon garlic powder

¼ teaspoon onion powder

1½ teaspoons nutritional yeast

Pinch of ground black pepper

Pinch of fine salt

Pinch of turmeric powder

FOR GARNISH

2 tablespoons microgreens

2 to 3 fresh chives, sliced

1 green onion, sliced

Coarse sea salt

1. Prepare the filling: Pour the oil into a medium-sized nonstick frying pan over medium heat. Add the onion and sauté for 3 minutes, or until turning translucent. Add the broccoli along with 1 tablespoon of water and the salt and pepper. Continue to cook for 3 to 4 minutes, until the broccoli is thawed. Remove from the pan and place in a bowl.

2. Prepare the omelette batter: Put all of the ingredients in a separate medium-sized bowl and whisk until a smooth batter has formed.

3. Lightly grease the same pan that you used to cook the filling with cooking spray and pour in the omelette batter. Cover and cook over medium heat for 8 minutes, then remove the lid and cook for 2 minutes more. When the omelette looks dry on top, the edges are slightly golden, and you can easily get the omelette to move, use a metal spatula to flip it over. Cook the other side for 5 minutes, uncovered.

4. Meanwhile, chop the broccoli into bite-sized pieces.

5. Top one half of the omelette with the broccoli filling and vegan cheese. Fold the other half over the filling to form the classic half-moon omelette shape.

6. Turn off the heat and cover the pan with a lid for 2 minutes to melt the vegan cheese.

7. Serve topped with the microgreens, chives, green onion, coarse salt, and some extra pepper.

biscuits and gravy

Yield: 6 servings

Prep Time: 10 minutes
(not including time to soak
cashews or make biscuits)

Cook Time: 10 minutes

Biscuits and gravy is a popular breakfast dish in the South. Fluffy biscuits are covered in a creamy white gravy that is traditionally filled with sausage. This vegan version uses textured vegetable protein (TVP) to replace the sausage. The creaminess of the gravy combined with the flaky layers of biscuits make this the perfect comforting breakfast. I like to get the biscuits into the oven and then make the gravy while they're baking.

1 cup (100g) textured vegetable protein

¾ cup (90g) raw cashews, soaked in water overnight and drained

2 cups (480ml) nondairy milk, divided

¼ Vidalia onion (about 2 ounces/ 55g), chopped

1 tablespoon olive oil

Leaves from 3 sprigs fresh thyme, plus more for garnish

1 teaspoon garlic powder

1 teaspoon onion powder

½ teaspoon salt

¼ teaspoon ground black pepper

¼ teaspoon dried parsley

2 teaspoons low-sodium soy sauce

¼ cup (30g) all-purpose flour

¼ cup (56g) vegan butter

1 batch Southern "Buttermilk" Biscuits (page 66)

1. Place the TVP in a bowl with 1 cup (240ml) of water. Set aside for 5 minutes to rehydrate.

2. Place the cashews and ¾ cup (180ml) of the nondairy milk in a high-powered blender. Blend on high speed for 1 to 2 minutes, until the cashew cream is thick and smooth. It will be slightly thicker than heavy cream.

3. In a large nonstick sauté pan or cast-iron skillet, sauté the onion in the olive oil over medium heat for 1 minute, or until just slightly softened.

4. Pour the rehydrated TVP into a wire strainer to drain any excess water, then add the TVP to the pan with the onion. Use a wooden spoon or rubber spatula to toss the ingredients together. Stir in the thyme, dried seasonings, and soy sauce and cook for 5 to 7 minutes, until the TVP starts to brown.

5. Sprinkle the flour over the TVP mixture and stir until the TVP is well coated in flour. Add the vegan butter and mix with the TVP until the butter has melted.

6. Reduce the heat to low. Pour in the cashew cream along with ½ cup (120ml) of the nondairy milk. Mix together and continue to add the remaining ¾ cup (180ml) of milk until the mixture is thick. Stir the gravy for 1 minute, until everything is well combined and the gravy is warm. Taste prior to serving and add more salt if needed.

7. Place 2 biscuits on a plate and top with some of the gravy, a few thyme leaves, and a pinch of pepper. Repeat with the remaining biscuits and gravy; enjoy warm.

breakfast burritos

Yield: 4 burritos (4 servings)
Prep Time: 15 minutes
Cook Time: 30 minutes

Breakfast burritos are one of my favorite foods. They are fun to make and can be great for meal prep! These burritos are filled with hash browns, a tofu scramble, a corn and pepper mixture, vegan cheddar, avocado, and a creamy Sriracha sauce. All of the flavors and textures work great together, but feel free to customize your burritos and add any other fillings you like.

HASH BROWNS

1 tablespoon olive oil

6 ounces (170g) frozen shredded hash browns

¼ teaspoon salt (omit if hash browns are salted)

CORN, ONION, AND PEPPERS

1½ teaspoons olive oil

⅓ cup (55g) frozen corn

¼ Vidalia onion (about 2 ounces/ 55g), chopped

½ orange bell pepper (about 2 ounces/55g), chopped

TOFU SCRAMBLE

1 tablespoon vegan butter

4 ounces (115g) firm tofu

¼ cup (60ml) nondairy milk

¼ teaspoon turmeric powder

¼ teaspoon garlic powder

Salt and pepper

¼ cup (28g) vegan cheddar shreds

CREAMY SRIRACHA SAUCE

¼ cup (60g) vegan sour cream

2 to 3 teaspoons Sriracha sauce

¼ cup (28g) vegan cheddar shreds

4 (8-inch/20cm) vegan flour tortillas

½ Hass avocado, thinly sliced

1. Prepare the hash browns: Pour the oil into a large nonstick frying pan, then add the hash browns and salt, if using. Pan-fry over medium-high heat for 10 minutes, or until the hash browns are golden brown, stirring occasionally to prevent sticking and burning. Transfer the hash browns to a bowl and set aside.

2. Prepare the corn, onion, and peppers: Lower the heat to medium and pour the oil into the same frying pan. Add the corn, onion, and bell pepper. Sauté for 5 minutes, or until the onion turns translucent. Use a spoon to transfer the vegetables to a bowl and set aside.

3. Prepare the tofu scramble: Reduce the heat to medium-low and melt the butter in the same frying pan. Use your hands to crumble the tofu directly into the pan. Add the nondairy milk and seasonings and stir with a wooden spoon or rubber spatula. Cook for 5 to 7 minutes, until the tofu has absorbed the milk. Add the vegan cheddar shreds and stir until melted. Remove the pan from the heat.

4. Prepare the creamy Sriracha sauce: In a medium-sized bowl, mix together the vegan sour cream and Sriracha. The sauce will be pale orange and smooth.

5. Assemble the burritos: Sprinkle 1 tablespoon of the vegan cheddar shreds across a tortilla, then add one-quarter of the tofu scramble, hash browns, and vegetable mixture. Top with one-quarter of the avocado slices and drizzle with about 2 teaspoons of the Sriracha sauce. Fold in both sides of the tortilla and then roll up the burrito; set aside. Repeat with the remaining tortillas and fillings.

6. Place a burrito in a panini press or on a small grill pan or frying pan. Cook for 2 to 3 minutes to help seal it up and make it golden brown. Repeat with the remaining burritos.

7. Serve with the remaining Sriracha sauce.

If you want to meal prep these burritos, I suggest leaving out the avocado because it will start to brown over time. To reheat the prepared burritos, simply place in the microwave for 1 to 2 minutes, until warmed through. If you prefer, you can prepare all of the components as directed in Steps 1 through 4 and store them in separate containers; when you're ready to eat, assemble and grill the burritos according to Steps 5 and 6.

coconut zucchini bread

Yield: one 9 by 5-inch (23 by 13cm) loaf (8 slices)

Prep Time: 15 minutes, plus time to cool

Cook Time: 55 minutes

Zucchini bread is something everyone needs to know how to make. In addition to being easy and delicious, it is a great way to sneak in some extra veggies! Don't worry, you can't taste the zucchini at all. The addition of coconut gives this version an incredible flavor and a bit of a tropical feel.

¾ cup (120g) grated zucchini

1½ cups (180g) all-purpose flour

⅓ cup (64g) organic cane sugar

⅓ cup (64g) organic dark brown sugar

2 teaspoons baking powder

½ teaspoon ground cinnamon

6 tablespoons (45g) sweetened shredded coconut, divided

½ cup (120ml) nondairy milk

1 egg replacer (see pages 11–12)

1 teaspoon vanilla extract

⅓ cup (80ml) vegetable oil

1. Preheat the oven to 350°F (176°C). Grease a 9 by 5-inch (23 by 13cm) loaf pan.

2. Wrap the grated zucchini in a clean kitchen towel and squeeze out the excess water using your hands.

3. In a large bowl, whisk together the flour, sugars, baking powder, cinnamon, and ¼ cup (30g) of the shredded coconut until well incorporated.

4. Mix in the zucchini, nondairy milk, egg replacer, vanilla extract, and oil using a spoon or rubber spatula. The batter will be thick.

5. Pour the batter into the prepared pan. Use a rubber spatula to smooth the top, then sprinkle with the remaining 2 tablespoons of shredded coconut.

6. Bake for 55 minutes, or until the bread is golden brown and a toothpick inserted in the center comes out almost clean with a slight bit of crumb on it. This will ensure that the bread is done but remains moist.

7. Let cool in the pan for at least 30 minutes before slicing. Using a serrated knife, cut into 8 equal slices.

2.

bites

I would be lying if I said this wasn't my favorite chapter in the book. It's all about starters, finger foods, and snacks—aka the best food. If you are having a party, going to a gathering, or just need something fun to make, this chapter has you covered. There are so many different flavors, different cuisines, and interesting things for you to try.

If you are looking for classic American comfort food, definitely check out the Southern "Buttermilk" Biscuits, the Popcorn Chick'n, or the Spinach and Artichoke Dip. If you're in the mood for something different, the Greek Nachos and the Sweet Gochujang Tempeh Bao are flavor explosions. But whatever you go with in this chapter is sure to make you happy!

arancini

Yield: 10 rice balls (5 servings)

Prep Time: 15 minutes, plus time to chill (not including time to make rice or tomato sauce)

Cook Time: 20 minutes

Arancini have always been a special treat in my family. My dad's mom—Mickey Grandma, as we called her—used to make them for Christmas and served them hot out of the oil. There was nothing better. Arancini, aka rice balls, are not hard to make at all and can be prepared with leftover or fresh rice. If using fresh rice as directed in this recipe, just allow it to cool completely before using it. The double breading makes these arancini extra crispy.

1 cup (160g) fine breadcrumbs

½ teaspoon paprika

¼ teaspoon dried parsley

¼ teaspoon salt

¼ teaspoon ground black pepper

¼ cup (30g) chickpea flour or all-purpose flour

½ cup (56g) vegan mozzarella shreds

½ batch Perfect White Rice (page 191)

1½ cups (350ml) canola or vegetable oil, for frying

FOR GARNISH

2 fresh basil leaves, chiffonaded

1 tablespoon shredded or grated vegan parmesan

1 teaspoon red pepper flakes (optional)

¼ cup (64g) Tomato Sauce (page 189), for dipping

1.   On a large plate, mix together the breadcrumbs and seasonings.

2.   In a medium-sized bowl, whisk the flour with ½ cup (120ml) of water to form a smooth batter.

3.   Put the vegan mozzarella shreds and cooked rice in a bowl and mix with a spoon. Scoop 2 tablespoons of the mixture into your hands and roll into a ball. Wetting your hands is helpful here. Repeat with the remaining rice mixture, making a total of 10 balls.

4.   Double-bread the rice balls: Put each ball in the batter, then roll in the seasoned breadcrumbs. Place back in the batter, then roll again in the breadcrumbs. Set the breaded balls on a plate.

5.   Refrigerate the balls for 1 hour or up to overnight. This ensures that everything will harden and the breading won't fall off when the balls are deep-fried.

6.   In a 1-quart (1L) saucepan, heat the oil over medium-high heat to 350°F (176°C). (Deep-frying in a smaller saucepan requires less oil and can be less intimidating.) The oil should be about 2 inches deep so that the rice balls are mostly covered when placed in the pan. Place 3 or 4 rice balls in the hot oil and fry for 6 minutes, or until golden, turning them every 2 minutes so they cook evenly on all sides. Remove from the oil with a slotted spoon or spider strainer and place on a paper towel–lined plate to drain. Repeat with the remaining rice balls.

7.   Top the arancini with the basil, vegan parmesan, and red pepper flakes, if desired, and serve immediately, with the tomato sauce on the side for dipping.

spinach *fritters*

Yield: 14 fritters (7 servings)
Prep Time: 10 minutes
Cook Time: 25 minutes

When I was younger, my great-grandma, whom I lovingly called Big Grandma, always made me these fritters. I gobbled them up because they were so good. These vegan fritters are a fun take on traditional fritters and are a great way to enjoy spinach.

½ onion, preferably Vidalia (about 4 ounces/115g), chopped

1 tablespoon olive oil

2 (16-ounce/454g) bags frozen chopped spinach, thawed

¼ cup (30g) flaxseed meal

½ cup (60g) all-purpose flour

1 tablespoon garlic powder

1 tablespoon onion powder

¼ teaspoon salt

¼ teaspoon ground black pepper, plus more for garnish

¼ teaspoon dried thyme leaves

½ cup (120ml) canola or vegetable oil, divided, for frying

2 sprigs fresh thyme, roughly chopped, for garnish

¼ teaspoon coarse sea salt, for garnish

1. In a large nonstick frying pan, cook the onion in the olive oil over medium-low heat for 5 minutes, or until translucent.

2. Meanwhile, wrap the thawed spinach in a paper towel and squeeze out the excess water. Place the spinach in a large bowl.

3. Prepare a flax egg by mixing the flaxseed meal with ¼ cup (60ml) of water in a small bowl. Set aside for 2 to 3 minutes to thicken.

4. Transfer the cooked onion to the bowl with the spinach. Add the flax egg, flour, and seasonings and mix with a spoon. The mixture should be sticky and should hold its shape if you scoop up a small portion. If it leaves your hands wet and will not hold its shape, mix in 1 to 2 tablespoons more flour; if it crumbles apart, mix in 1 to 2 tablespoons of water.

5. Wipe the frying pan clean and set it over medium heat. Pour in ¼ cup (60ml) of the canola oil and allow it warm up for 1 minute. (If you don't have a large frying pan and you need to cook the fritters in three batches rather than two, use 2¼ tablespoons of oil per batch.)

6. Scoop up 2 heaping tablespoons of the spinach mixture and use your hands to form it into a patty 2 to 3 inches in diameter and about ½ inch (13mm) thick. Make 6 more patties, then place the 7 patties in the oil and pan-fry for 4 to 5 minutes per side, until golden brown; the spinach will turn dark green. Remove the fritters to a paper towel–lined plate to drain.

7. Repeat with the remaining ¼ cup (60ml) of oil and remaining spinach mixture, making a total of 14 patties.

8. Serve warm, topped with the fresh thyme, coarse salt, and extra pepper.

betty grandma's meatballs

Yield: 20 meatballs
(5 to 10 servings)

Prep Time: 20 minutes

Cook Time: 45 minutes

Betty Grandma, one of my great-grandmas, was a tiny woman who cooked better than any restaurant chef. (That's her pan in the photo.) She made tiny little meatballs that were crispy on the outside and served without sauce. This vegan version uses textured vegetable protein to mimic ground meat; the artichoke hearts help provide a meatiness as well. These meatballs should be enjoyed hot out of the frying pan, where they develop an extra-crispy outer layer. The number of servings varies depending on whether you'll be offering them as part of a large appetizer spread or serving them as a hearty starter course.

2 cups (200g) textured vegetable protein (TVP)

1¾ cups (415ml) low-sodium vegetable broth, heated

1 (14-ounce/396g) can artichoke hearts, drained

½ cup (80g) fine breadcrumbs, plus more if needed, divided

½ cup (56g) shredded or grated vegan parmesan, divided

2 tablespoons low-sodium soy sauce

1 tablespoon garlic powder

1 tablespoon onion powder

1½ teaspoons dried parsley

¼ teaspoon ground black pepper

¼ cup (60ml) olive oil, divided

2 leaves fresh basil, chiffonaded, for garnish

1. Preheat the oven to 375°F (190°C).

2. Put the TVP in a bowl and pour the hot broth over it. Mix together and let sit for 10 minutes to rehydrate. The TVP will absorb the liquid and expand.

3. Put the rehydrated TVP, artichoke hearts, ¼ cup (40g) of the breadcrumbs, ¼ cup (28g) of the vegan parmesan, the soy sauce, garlic powder, onion powder, parsley, and pepper in a food processor and pulse on high speed until the ingredients are well combined and the artichoke hearts are broken down. The mixture should stick together and be easily formed into a ball. If it seems overly sticky or is leaving your hand wet, add 1 to 2 tablespoons of breadcrumbs; if it seems dry and is crumbling, add 1 to 2 tablespoons of water. Taste the mixture and adjust the seasoning to your preference.

4. Pour 2 tablespoons of the oil onto a rimmed baking sheet, coating the bottom of the pan.

5. On a plate, mix together the remaining ¼ cup (40g) of the breadcrumbs and remaining ¼ cup (28g) of the vegan parmesan.

6. Scoop 2 tablespoons of the TVP mixture and roll into a ball using your hands, then roll the ball in the breadcrumb mixture. Place on the prepared baking sheet. If you are having difficulty rolling the mixture into balls, lightly wet your hands. Repeat until all of the meatballs have been made; you will get a total of 20 meatballs.

7. Bake the meatballs for 20 minutes, then flip them over and bake for another 20 minutes, until golden brown.

8. Pour the remaining 2 tablespoons of oil into an extra-large frying pan. Pan-fry the meatballs over medium heat for 5 minutes, shaking the pan occasionally.

9. Serve immediately, garnished with the basil.

greek nachos

Yield: 4 to 6 servings

Prep Time: 30 minutes, plus time to chill tzatziki

Here, Greek flavors and ingredients are used to create a fun twist on classic nachos. These cold nachos are topped with a homemade vegan tzatziki and some fresh vegetables and pack a ton of flavor. They are great for a backyard party and are definitely meant to be shared. The tzatziki can be made a day ahead. If you have some left over, you can refrigerate it for up to 3 days.

VEGAN TZATZIKI

1 cucumber, preferably English (about 8 ounces/225g)

1 (16-ounce/454g) block silken tofu

4 cloves garlic, minced

Juice of ½ lemon

1 tablespoon apple cider vinegar

1 teaspoon red wine vinegar

½ teaspoon salt

Fronds from 4 sprigs fresh dill, chopped

1 (7⅓-ounce/207g) bag pita chips

1 (2¼-ounce/64g) can sliced black olives

½ cup (100g) canned chickpeas, drained and rinsed

½ red onion (about 4 ounces/ 115g), diced

FOR GARNISH

Leaves from 3 sprigs fresh parsley, roughly chopped

Fronds from 2 sprigs fresh dill, roughly chopped

1 or 2 lemon slices

Coarse sea salt

Ground black pepper

1. Cut the cucumber in half. Using a food processor or box grater, grate one half of the cucumber. Wrap the grated cucumber in a clean kitchen towel and squeeze out the excess water. Place in a medium-sized bowl.

2. Prepare the tzatziki: Place the tofu, garlic, lemon juice, vinegars, and salt in a blender. Blend until smooth and liquefied. Pour the blended mixture into the bowl with the grated cucumber and add the dill. Mix with a spoon until well combined. Place in the refrigerator to thicken for 20 minutes or overnight.

3. Dice the remaining half of the cucumber.

4. Assemble the nachos: Place the pita chips on a large plate or a serving dish. Arrange the black olives, chickpeas, diced cucumber, and red onion on top. You can either place the toppings in neat sections or scatter them over the chips.

5. Drizzle half of the tzatziki over the nachos and use the remainder for dipping. Garnish the nachos with the parsley, dill, lemon slice(s), salt, and pepper.

vegetable spring rolls

Yield: 12 spring rolls
(3 to 4 servings)

Prep Time: 15 minutes

Cook Time: 35 minutes

Homemade spring rolls are a real treat. This fun appetizer has a crispy, thin outer layer filled with vegetables and tofu. Making your own wrappers is not hard at all, but if you're lucky enough to find spring roll pastry in your grocery store (see note, opposite), you can use that to eliminate a few steps. Either way, you are going to end up with something delicious.

WRAPPERS

1½ cups (180g) all-purpose flour

1 tablespoon cornstarch, plus more for dusting

¼ teaspoon salt

1 teaspoon canola or vegetable oil

FILLING

6 cups (170g) shredded cabbage blend

6 ounces (170g) firm tofu, diced

2 cloves garlic, minced

2 green onions, chopped

1 tablespoon low-sodium soy sauce

2 teaspoons Sriracha sauce

1 teaspoon maple syrup

Pinch of salt

1 to 3 tablespoons canola or vegetable oil, for frying

Sliced green onions, for garnish

White sesame seeds, for garnish

Sweet chili sauce, low-sodium soy sauce, or other sauce of choice, for dipping

1. Prepare the wrappers: In a large bowl, whisk together the flour, cornstarch, and salt. Pour in the oil and 1½ cups (350ml) of water. Whisk until smooth. The batter will be very thin.

2. Use a silicone brush to brush about 2 tablespoons of the batter in a very thin layer over the bottom of a medium-sized nonstick frying pan. Make sure there are no spots without batter; if there are, simply brush a little bit of batter over the top. Cook the wrapper over very low heat for 1 to 2 minutes, until the edges begin to curl up. Put the wrapper on a plate and lightly dust the top with cornstarch to prevent sticking as you layer the cooked wrappers. Repeat with the remaining batter; you should get a total of 12 wrappers.

3. Prepare the filling: Put the cabbage and ½ cup (120ml) of water in a large frying pan over medium heat. Cover with a lid and steam for 7 minutes, until the cabbage has softened. Check it occasionally to make sure there is enough water to keep the cabbage from burning; add more water if needed. Once the cabbage has softened, add the remaining ingredients for the filling and cook for 5 minutes to warm everything through.

4. To assemble the spring rolls, place a wrapper on a clean work surface. Scoop 2 tablespoons of the filling onto the bottom half of the wrapper in a log shape. Fold the two outer sides of the circle inward to cover the outer edges of the filling. Fold the bottom edge, closest to you, over the two folded-in sides and roll up the wrapper to complete the roll. Place the roll seam side down on a plate and repeat with the remaining wrappers and filling.

5. Fry the spring rolls: Heat the oil in a large frying pan over medium heat for 1 minute. When the oil is hot, place the spring rolls in the pan without touching and pan-fry for 7 minutes, or until golden brown. If working in batches, use an additional 1 to 2 tablespoons of oil as needed.

6. Garnish with sliced green onions and sesame seeds. Enjoy warm with your choice of dipping sauce.

If using store-bought spring roll pastry wrappers for this recipe, purchase 8-inch (20cm) square ones. To roll them, follow the instructions in Step 4. If you want to freeze the spring rolls after they have been fried, allow them to cool. Place them on a rimmed baking sheet or tray and put it in the freezer for 1 hour to freeze them individually before transferring them to a zip-top plastic bag or other freezer-safe storage container. To reheat and recrisp them, remove from the freezer and place directly in a preheated 375°F (196°C) oven for 7 to 10 minutes.

hummus-stuffed falafel

Yield: 14 stuffed falafel (4 to 6 servings)

Prep Time: 30 minutes, plus time to chill hummus and falafel mixture

Cook Time: 15 minutes

Inspired by an idea from a very good friend, this falafel is a fun twist on tradition. Falafel has been a godsend for vegans and vegetarians for a long time. Homemade falafel is actually pretty easy to make, but this recipe takes it one step further and fills the falafel with hummus. As you bite into them, you get a burst of warm hummus. Homemade hummus is quick to prepare, but if you don't feel like making it yourself, you can always use store-bought. You will need about ⅓ cup (100g).

HUMMUS

1 cup (250g) canned chickpeas, drained and rinsed

Juice of ½ lemon

2 cloves garlic, peeled

2½ tablespoons tahini

¼ teaspoon fine salt, or to taste

1 tablespoon olive oil

FALAFEL

2 cups (500g) canned chickpeas, drained and rinsed

1 teaspoon baking powder

1 teaspoon ground cumin

Pinch of ground black pepper

20 sprigs fresh parsley (about 3 ounces/85g)

Juice of ½ lemon

¼ teaspoon fine salt

⅓ onion, preferably Vidalia (about 3 ounces/85g), roughly chopped

2 cups (475ml) canola or vegetable oil, for frying

FOR GARNISH

Coarse sea salt

Lemon slices

Fresh parsley sprigs

1. Make the hummus: Put all of the ingredients plus ⅓ cup (80ml) of water in a food processor and process on high speed for about 5 minutes, until very smooth and creamy. Scrape down the sides as needed to make sure everything is getting evenly broken down. Transfer to a container and place in the freezer for 15 to 20 minutes, until thickened but not frozen.

2. Prepare the falafel: In the food processor, pulse all of the ingredients on high speed for about 1 minute. The chickpeas will break down, becoming somewhat crumbly and pastelike. Don't overprocess; otherwise, the mixture will turn into hummus. Transfer to a bowl, cover, and place the falafel mixture in the refrigerator to chill for at least 15 minutes.

3. When you're ready to cook the falafel, heat the canola oil in a 1-quart (1L) saucepan over medium heat to 350°F (176°C). (Deep-frying in a smaller saucepan requires less oil and can be less intimidating.) The oil should be about 2 inches (5cm) deep so that the falafel are mostly covered when placed in the pan.

4. While the oil is heating, form the stuffed falafel balls: Scoop 2 tablespoons of the falafel mixture into your hand and shape it into a patty. Then scoop 1 teaspoon of the hummus into the middle. Lift the sides of the patty up and over the hummus, pinch it together at the top, and roll it into a ball between your hands, sealing the hummus inside. Repeat with the remaining falafel mixture and hummus, making a total of 14 stuffed balls. You will have leftover hummus for dipping.

5. Place 4 or 5 falafel in the hot oil and deep-fry for 5 minutes, or until golden brown, turning them once during frying so that they brown evenly on all sides. When done, use a slotted spoon or spider strainer to remove the falafel from the oil and place on a paper towel–lined plate to drain. Repeat with the remaining falafel.

You will need four 15½-ounce (439g) cans of chickpeas for this recipe.

6. Transfer the falafel to a serving plate, sprinkle with coarse salt, and decorate the plate with lemon slices and parsley sprigs. Serve with the remaining hummus.

mozzarella in carrozza

Yield: 2 sandwiches

Prep Time: 5 minutes (not including time to make vegan mozzarella or tomato sauce)

Cook Time: 8 minutes

Don't call this grilled cheese. Well, technically, I suppose it is, but it's so much more than that. Mozzarella in carrozza is a cross between a grilled cheese sandwich and a fried mozzarella stick. The bread is coated in a layer of breadcrumbs and then quickly pan-fried. The vegan cheese is gooey and melty, making this the perfect snack.

¼ cup (40g) fine breadcrumbs

¼ teaspoon dried parsley

¼ teaspoon paprika

Pinch of salt

Pinch of ground black pepper

¼ cup (30g) all-purpose flour

3 tablespoons olive oil

½ cup (135g) Homemade Vegan Mozzarella (page 190)

4 slices white bread

¼ cup (64g) Tomato Sauce (page 189), warmed, for dipping

1. Mix together the breadcrumbs, parsley, paprika, salt, and pepper on a plate.

2. In a large bowl (it should be big enough to fit the slices of bread), whisk the flour with ¼ cup (60ml) of water to form a batter.

3. Pour the oil into a sauté pan or large frying pan and warm it over low heat while you prepare the sandwiches. (If your pan isn't big enough to fit both sandwiches, heat up only 1½ tablespoons of the oil and pan-fry one sandwich at a time.)

4. To assemble the sandwiches, scoop ¼ cup (65g) of vegan mozzarella onto a slice of bread and spread it with a knife. Place another slice of bread on top. Dip both sides of the sandwich into the batter, allowing the excess to drip off. Then coat both sides in the breadcrumb mixture. Place the sandwich in the pan. Repeat to make the second sandwich.

5. Increase the heat to medium and pan-fry the sandwiches for 3 to 4 minutes per side, until golden and crispy.

6. Cut the sandwiches in half diagonally and serve with the tomato sauce for dipping.

popcorn chick'n

Yield: 4 to 6 servings

Prep Time: 15 minutes

Cook Time: 30 minutes

In this recipe, bite-sized pieces of tofu are coated in a crispy, flaky breading and then deep-fried to a beautiful golden color. The batter mixes with the flour to create that perfect crunch. Don't be afraid if a little batter drips into your breading; it will just make everything better. This chick'n is great dipped in just about any sauce, but vegan ranch (page 187) is my favorite.

1 (16-ounce/454g) block super-firm (high-protein) tofu

BATTER

⅔ cup (80g) all-purpose flour

⅔ cup (160ml) nondairy milk

Pinch of salt

Pinch of ground black pepper

BREADING

½ cup (60g) all-purpose flour

1 tablespoon garlic powder

1 tablespoon onion powder

1 tablespoon paprika

1 teaspoon chili powder

¼ teaspoon salt

¼ teaspoon ground black pepper

1½ cups (350ml) canola or vegetable oil, for frying

Ground black pepper, for garnish (optional)

Sliced green onions, for garnish (optional)

1. Cut the block of tofu lengthwise into thirds to create 3 large rectangles of equal size. Using your hands, break each rectangle into 20 bite-sized pieces, giving you 60 pieces of tofu.

2. Prepare the batter: Whisk together the flour, nondairy milk, salt, and pepper in a medium-sized bowl.

3. Prepare the breading: Place all of the ingredients on a large plate and mix with a fork.

4. In a 1-quart (1L) saucepan, heat the oil to 350°F (176°C) over medium heat. (Deep-frying in a smaller saucepan requires less oil and can be less intimidating.) The oil should be about 2 inches (5cm) deep so that the tofu is mostly covered in oil.

5. While the oil is heating, bread the tofu: Dip 5 pieces of tofu into the batter, then remove, allowing the excess batter to drip off. Transfer the coated pieces to the plate with the breading and coat them well. Place on a separate plate until ready to fry. Repeat with the remaining tofu, batter, and breading.

6. When the oil is hot, add 10 pieces of tofu and fry for about 5 minutes, until golden and crispy. Use a slotted spoon or spider strainer to remove from the oil and place on a paper towel–lined plate to drain. (If desired, transfer the completed tofu to a 300°F [158C°] oven to keep warm while you fry the rest of the tofu.) Repeat until all of the tofu is fried.

7. Serve hot, garnished with pepper and sliced green onions, if desired.

vegan cheddar and potato pierogi

Yield: 4 to 6 servings

Prep Time: 30 minutes, plus time to chill dough

Cook Time: 1 hour 10 minutes

If you have never eaten pierogi, you are in for a treat. While these require a little bit of patience and love, there is nothing better than creamy, cheesy mashed potatoes inside a dumpling. This is a fun recipe to get someone else involved in. Pierogi can be boiled or pan-fried, but trust me, the pan-fried way is definitely tastier. These pierogi can also be frozen (see note, opposite).

DOUGH

3½ cups (420g) all-purpose flour, plus more for dusting

3 tablespoons olive oil

¼ teaspoon salt

1 large onion, preferably Vidalia (about 10 ounces/285g), sliced

FILLING

2 russet potatoes (about 1½ pounds/680g), peeled and quartered

¼ cup (60ml) nondairy milk

¼ cup (60g) vegan sour cream

3 tablespoons vegan butter

½ teaspoon salt

6 ounces (170g) vegan cheddar shreds

4 tablespoons (56g) vegan butter, divided

2 ounces (55g) vegan cheddar shreds, for serving

Thinly sliced fresh chives, for garnish (optional)

½ cup (120g) vegan sour cream, for serving

1. Prepare the dough: Sift the flour into a large bowl. Add the oil, salt, and 1 cup (240ml) of warm water. Mix with a fork until a shaggy dough comes together. Dump out the dough onto a clean, lightly floured surface. Knead by hand for 3 to 5 minutes, until smooth. Form it into a ball, cover with plastic wrap, and place in the refrigerator to chill for 30 minutes.

2. Caramelize the onion: In a medium-sized nonstick frying pan, cook the onion with 1 cup (240ml) of water over medium-low heat. When the water has evaporated, add another 1 cup (240ml) of water. The onion will go from white to light brown to a darker brown color. Continue adding ¼ cup (60ml) of water at a time until it reaches the level of caramelization you prefer. This process should take about 30 minutes.

3. Prepare the filling: In a medium-sized saucepan, boil the potatoes uncovered over high heat for 15 to 20 minutes, until fork-tender. Drain. Add the nondairy milk, vegan sour cream, vegan butter, and salt. Mash with a fork or potato masher until smooth. Fold in the vegan cheddar.

4. After 30 minutes, remove the dough from the refrigerator. On a clean, lightly floured surface, roll out the dough to ¼ inch (6mm) thick. Using a round cookie cutter, biscuit cutter, or glass, cut out 3½-inch (9cm) circles. Place them on a clean, floured section of your counter or a floured cookie sheet; do not stack them on a plate, as they will stick. Cover the dough with a clean kitchen towel to prevent it from drying out. Reroll the scraps and repeat the process until all of the dough is used; you will end up with about 24 circles.

5. Place 2 heaping tablespoons of the potato filling on the bottom half of a dough circle. Wet the other half of the circle with water and then fold the dough over the filling to form a half moon. Pinch the edges to seal. Place on a dish and keep the pierogi covered. Repeat until all of the pierogi are made.

Caramelizing the onions in water
is healthier than the traditional
method using oil or fat, but equally
delicious.

You can freeze the uncooked pierogi.
After completing Step 5, freeze
them individually for 1 to 2 hours.
Then, once hardened, transfer them
to a zip-top plastic bag or other
freezer-safe storage container.
To cook from frozen, thaw in the
refrigerator overnight, then pick up
with Step 6. Leftover cooked pierogi
will keep in the refrigerator for up
to 2 days.

6.   Fill a large pot with 3½ to 4 quarts (3.5 to 4L) of salted
water and bring to a boil over high heat. When the water is
boiling, add 6 pierogi and cook for 3 to 5 minutes, until they
float to the top. Remove with a slotted spoon and put on a
cookie sheet or plate; try not to let them overlap. Repeat with
the remaining pierogi.

7.   After all of the pierogi are boiled, melt 1 tablespoon of
the vegan butter in a large nonstick frying pan over medium
heat. Add one-quarter of the boiled pierogi and pan-fry for 3
minutes per side, or until crispy and golden. Remove to a plate
and repeat with the remaining butter and pierogi.

8.   Sprinkle the pierogi with the caramelized onions and
vegan cheddar and garnish with fresh chives, if desired. Serve
with the vegan sour cream.

southern "buttermilk" biscuits

Yield: 12 biscuits
Prep Time: 20 minutes
Cook Time: 20 minutes

Homemade vegan biscuits are easier to make than you would probably expect. They require only a few ingredients and come out so flaky. The most important thing to remember is to keep your nondairy milk and vegan butter very, very cold. You can even place the butter in the freezer for a half hour before using it. Grating the butter helps it mix more easily into the dough. These biscuits freeze nicely after they are baked (see note, opposite). I enjoy serving them with dinner as you might serve rolls—especially for a holiday meal! Of course, they also pair well with jam and butter for breakfast or afternoon tea.

1 cup (240ml) cold nondairy milk

1 tablespoon apple cider vinegar

2½ cups (300g) all-purpose flour, plus more for dusting

2 tablespoons baking powder

½ teaspoon organic granulated sugar

¼ teaspoon salt

½ cup (112g) cold vegan butter

1. Preheat the oven to 450°F (232°C). Line a 9 by 13-inch (23 by 33cm) or similar size rimmed baking sheet with parchment paper.

2. Prepare the vegan buttermilk: Mix together the nondairy milk and vinegar in a medium-sized glass bowl. Set aside in the refrigerator for 5 minutes. The milk will curdle.

3. Meanwhile, put the flour, baking powder, sugar, and salt in a large bowl. Whisk to break up any clumps.

4. Make a well in the middle of the flour mixture and pour in the vegan buttermilk. Using a rubber spatula, gently move the flour around to absorb the liquid. It is important to be gentle with the dough.

5. Using a box grater, grate the vegan butter into the bowl with the dough. It will look like shredded cheese. Gently mix the butter into the dough for about 3 minutes, just until the dough starts to stick to itself and pull away from the sides of the bowl. Do not overmix.

6. Flour a clean work surface and dump out the dough onto the floured surface. Using your hands, gently work the dough into a rectangle about 5 by 7 inches (13 by 18cm) and ½ inch (13mm) thick, with a short end facing you.

7. Fold the dough in half by taking the short edge closest to you and folding it upward to meet the top edge. Use your hands to gently press the dough together until it is ½ to 1 inch (13mm to 2.5cm) thick.

8. Pick up the dough and rotate it clockwise 90 degrees so the folded edge is on the left side and the dough resembles a closed book. Repeat the process of bringing the edge of the dough closest to you upward to meet the top edge. Gently press the dough until it is ½ to 1 inch (13mm to 2.5cm) thick.

To freeze, allow the biscuits to cool for about an hour. Place the biscuits in the freezer, lying flat in a single layer, not touching, for an hour, or until they've hardened. When the biscuits have hardened, put them in a zip-top plastic bag or other freezer-safe storage container. To reheat from frozen, pop them in a preheated 450°F (232°C) oven for 7 to 10 minutes, until warmed through.

9. Repeat Step 8 two more times. Always rotate the dough 90 degrees so you are not folding the same side you just worked on. This is what gives the biscuits flaky layers.

10. Form the dough into one final rectangle about 7 by 12 inches (18 by 30cm) and ½ inch (13mm) thick.

11. Using a lightly floured 2¾-inch (7cm) biscuit cutter or mason jar lid, begin to cut out the biscuits. Place on the prepared baking sheet, making sure they are all touching. This helps them rise and bake more evenly. Rework the scraps into another smaller rectangle that is about ½ inch (13mm) thick. Cut out more biscuits and place on the baking sheet. Repeat until all of the dough has been used.

12. Bake for 18 to 20 minutes, or until the biscuits are golden brown. Allow to cool on the pan for 5 minutes before serving.

spinach
and artichoke dip

Yield: 4 to 6 servings
Prep Time: 10 minutes
Cook Time: 35 minutes

I used to love going to restaurants with my family and getting a hot, bubbling dish of spinach and artichoke dip. It is salty, tangy, and creamy, making it the perfect appetizer. This vegan version is a fun dish to share and is best enjoyed while hot and bubbly. Serve it with crusty bread, crackers, or your favorite vegetables.

1 (16-ounce/454g) bag frozen chopped spinach, thawed

2 cloves garlic, minced

1 (14-ounce/396g) can artichoke hearts, drained and chopped

1 (8-ounce/227g) tub vegan cream cheese

½ cup (120g) vegan sour cream

½ cup (56g) shredded or grated vegan parmesan, divided

1 cup (112g) vegan mozzarella shreds, divided

Pinch of salt

Pinch of ground black pepper

1. Preheat the oven to 350°F (176°C).

2. Wrap the thawed spinach in a paper towel and squeeze out the excess water. This step is very important; if the spinach is too watery, the dip will be less creamy.

3. In a large bowl, mix together the spinach, garlic, artichoke hearts, vegan cream cheese, vegan sour cream, half of the vegan parmesan, half of the vegan mozzarella shreds, and the salt and pepper until well combined. Transfer the mixture to an 8-inch (20cm) square baking dish and sprinkle the remaining vegan parmesan and vegan mozzarella shreds over the top.

4. Bake for 25 to 30 minutes, until bubbling, then broil on high for 5 minutes to brown the top slightly. Serve warm.

sweet gochujang
tempeh bao

Yield: 12 bao (4 to 6 servings)

Prep Time: 30 minutes, plus time for dough to rise and buns to proof

Cook Time: 45 minutes

Homemade bao are truly a treat. These soft and fluffy buns are a little bit sweet and so delicious. Filled with a sweet and spicy tempeh and crunchy vegetables, they make a wonderful snack or light lunch. A steamer basket is essential for this recipe; they are easy to find online and pretty inexpensive.

BUNS

⅓ cup (80ml) nondairy milk

1 (¼-ounce/7g) packet active dry yeast

1½ tablespoons organic granulated sugar, divided

2½ cups (300g) all-purpose flour, plus more for dusting

1 teaspoon baking powder

½ teaspoon salt

2 tablespoons plus ½ teaspoon avocado or vegetable oil, divided, plus more for brushing

SWEET GOCHUJANG TEMPEH

1 (8-ounce/224g) package tempeh

2 teaspoons avocado or vegetable oil

2 tablespoons gochujang paste

1 tablespoon maple syrup

1½ teaspoons low-sodium soy sauce

¼ teaspoon garlic powder

6 cups (170g) shredded cabbage blend

1 carrot (about 2 ounces/55g), peeled into ribbons or julienned

½ cucumber, preferably English (about 4 ounces/115g), julienned

3 green onions, sliced, for garnish

1 tablespoon sesame seeds, for garnish

1. Prepare the buns: Heat the nondairy milk to 100°F to 110°F (37°C to 43°C). Mix the warm milk with the yeast and ½ tablespoon of the sugar. Set aside to proof for 10 minutes, until foamy.

2. In a large bowl, whisk together the flour, baking powder, salt, and remaining 1 tablespoon of sugar. Pour in the proofed yeast mixture, 3 tablespoons of water, and 2 tablespoons of the oil. Mix with a rubber spatula until the dough begins to come together.

3. Dump the dough out onto a clean, very lightly floured surface and knead with your hands for 5 to 7 minutes, until it forms a smooth ball. Brush the bowl with the remaining ½ teaspoon of oil and put the dough back in the bowl. Cover with a clean kitchen towel and set aside to rise for 1 hour. (It will not double in size.)

4. After the dough has risen, remove it from the bowl and place it on a clean surface. Use a rolling pin to roll out the dough to ¼ inch (6mm) thick. Use a 3½-inch (9cm) biscuit cutter or glass to cut out circles, gathering up the scraps and rerolling the dough as needed, until you have a total of 12 dough circles.

5. Lightly brush the tops of the dough circles with oil and fold in half. Then very gently roll the buns to elongate them into a slightly oval shape. Place on a rimmed baking sheet, cover with the towel, and allow to rise for 45 minutes.

6. About 20 minutes before the buns are done rising, prepare the tempeh: Use a sharp knife to cut the tempeh crosswise into 15 rectangles. Then cut each rectangle in half, giving you 30 small tempeh squares. Place the tempeh in a large nonstick frying pan with ½ cup (120ml) of water. Cover with a lid and steam the tempeh over medium-high heat for 15 minutes, or until it looks a bit puffy and all of the water has been absorbed. Reduce the heat to medium and pour in the oil; sauté for 5 to 7 minutes, until the tempeh is golden and crispy.

SPECIAL EQUIPMENT:
Large two-tiered bamboo
steamer

7.   In a small bowl, mix together the gochujang paste, maple syrup, soy sauce, garlic powder, and 1½ teaspoons of water to form a thick sauce. Pour it over the tempeh and cook for 1 minute, tossing to coat the pieces evenly with the sauce.

8.   Line both steamer baskets with parchment paper, then place 4 buns in each basket. Bring a sauté pan or wok filled with 6 cups (1.5L) of water to a boil over high heat. Reduce the heat to medium to maintain a vigorous simmer and place one steamer basket in the pan. Cover with the lid and steam the buns for 10 minutes. The buns will appear shiny on the outside and will have increased slightly in size. Do not open the steamer to check on them. Remove from the heat and carefully take the buns out. They will be very hot. Repeat with the 4 remaining uncooked buns.

9.   To assemble the bao: Open the buns and place a few pieces of cabbage, carrot, and cucumber along with 2 or 3 pieces of tempeh in each. Sprinkle with the green onions and sesame seeds and serve.

onion rings

Yield: 4 to 6 servings
Prep Time: 20 minutes
Cook Time: 25 minutes

Crunchy, crispy onion rings are an American classic. They are easy to make at home and very delicious. Deep-frying doesn't have to be intimidating, so don't be nervous; it is actually much easier than it may seem. These onion rings pair nicely with my Meaty Vegan Burgers (page 118) and my Buffalo Chick'n Sandwiches (page 108). Serve them with ketchup, vegan ranch (page 187), or your favorite dipping sauce. You can freeze any leftovers (see note below).

BATTER

1¼ cups (150g) all-purpose flour

¼ teaspoon baking powder

¼ teaspoon paprika

¼ teaspoon salt

¼ teaspoon ground black pepper

1¼ cups (300ml) sparkling water

BREADING

1½ cups (240g) fine breadcrumbs

½ teaspoon paprika

½ teaspoon salt

¼ teaspoon ground black pepper

3 cups (710ml) canola or vegetable oil, plus more if needed, for frying

3 large sweet onions, such as Vidalia (about 1½ pounds/680g), cut crosswise into ½-inch (13mm)-thick slices

Coarse sea salt, for sprinkling

1.   Prepare the batter: Whisk together all of the ingredients in a large bowl. The mixture will be slightly thinner than pancake batter.

2.   Prepare the breading: Mix all of the ingredients with a fork in a second large bowl.

3.   Heat the oil in a 2-quart (2L) saucepan over medium heat to 350°F (176°C). The oil should be about 5 inches (12.7cm) deep so that the onion rings will be fully submerged.

4.   Separate the onion slices into individual rings. Dip the onion rings into the batter. Allow any excess batter to drip off, then coat the onion rings in the breading.

5.   When the oil is hot, add 7 or 8 onion rings and fry for 3 minutes, or until golden brown. Use a slotted spoon or spider strainer to remove from the oil and place on a paper towel–lined plate to drain. Repeat with the remaining onion rings. If you need to add more oil during the frying process, allow it to come to temperature before adding more onion rings.

6.   Sprinkle the onion rings with coarse salt and serve warm.

To freeze leftover onion rings, arrange them in a single layer on a rimmed baking sheet or tray. Place in the freezer for 1 to 2 hours, until hardened, then transfer to a zip-top plastic bag or other freezer-safe storage container. When ready to eat them, bake them straight from the freezer in a preheated 425°F (218°C) oven for 6 to 8 minutes, until warm.

72   2. Bites

vegetable dumplings

Yield: 40 dumplings
(6 to 8 servings)

Prep Time: 45 minutes

Cook Time: 17 minutes

Homemade dumplings are some of my favorite things to make. Regardless of how well you can shape a dumpling, they will always taste delicious. Here, soft wrappers with crispy, golden bottoms are stuffed with a delicious veggie filling. These are fun to make with loved ones, and teaming up on the work helps the process go by much quicker. There are a bunch of ways to pleat dumplings, so if you have trouble doing it the way I describe here, just do whatever you can based on your skill level.

WRAPPERS

3 cups (360g) all-purpose flour, plus more for dusting

¼ teaspoon salt

FILLING

1 (14-ounce/397g) block firm tofu

5 cups (140g) shredded cabbage blend

2 carrots (about 4 ounces/115g), peeled

4 green onions, chopped

1 (1-inch/2.5cm) piece ginger, peeled

1 teaspoon garlic powder

1½ tablespoons low-sodium soy sauce

2 tablespoons toasted sesame oil, for the pan

1 green onion, sliced, for garnish

1 tablespoon black sesame seeds, for garnish

1 tablespoon white sesame seeds, for garnish

¼ cup (60ml) low-sodium soy sauce, for dipping

1.   Prepare the wrappers: Whisk the flour and salt in a large bowl. Slowly pour in ½ cup (120ml) of warm water while mixing. Mix with a fork until the dough turns shaggy and rough, then turn the dough onto a clean work surface and knead with your hands for about 5 minutes. The dough will become smooth and form a ball. If it feels too dry, add 1 tablespoon of water at a time until the dough is smooth.

2.   Divide the dough in half and form each half into a ball. Punch a hole in the middle of each ball and form it into a donut shape that is about 7 inches (18cm) in diameter and 1 inch (2.5cm) thick. Cover the dough with a clean kitchen towel and let it rest for 15 minutes.

3.   Meanwhile, prepare the filling: Place all of the ingredients in a food processor and pulse on high speed for about 3 minutes, until everything is chopped into small pieces. Continue pulsing until the mixture has the consistency of a rough paste; this sticky texture will help the filling adhere to the wrappers.

4.   Cut the dumpling wrapper "donuts" in half, giving you 4 long strips of equal length. Cut each strip into 10 pieces, about 1 inch (2.5cm) long. You will have 40 pieces of dough.

5.   Cover the cut pieces with the towel. It is important to keep the dough covered so it doesn't dry out.

6.   Lightly flour a clean work surface and a rolling pin. Take a dough piece and roll it out into a very thin 4-inch (10cm) circle. Scoop up 1 tablespoon of the filling and place it on one half of the circle. Lightly wet the other half of the circle with water. Fold the wrapper in half like a taco, then use your fingers to pleat the dumpling and pinch it shut. Place on a plate and cover. Repeat until all of the dumplings are filled and sealed.

The uncooked dumplings can be frozen after Step 6 and then cooked later, directly from frozen, as directed in Steps 7 and 8. They can also be frozen after being cooked and warmed in a skillet with 2 tablespoons of water over medium heat. Make sure to freeze the dumplings individually for about 1 hour, spread out on a rimmed baking sheet or tray, before transferring them to a zip-top plastic bag or other freezer-safe storage container.

7. In an extra-large (15-inch/38cm or larger) nonstick frying pan, heat the oil over medium heat for 1 minute. Arrange the dumplings in a circular pattern in the pan. They can be very close together, but do not let them touch, as they will grow while they steam. If your pan isn't big enough, cook the dumplings in 2 batches using 1 tablespoon of oil per batch.

8. Increase the heat to medium-high and pan-fry the dumplings for 5 to 7 minutes, until the bottoms turn golden and crispy. Then pour ¼ cup (60ml) of water over the dumplings and cover the pan with a lid. Steam over medium heat for 10 minutes, or until the water is absorbed. (If cooking them in 2 batches, use 2 tablespoons of water per batch.)

9. When the dumplings are done, garnish with the green onion slices and sesame seeds. Serve with the soy sauce for dipping.

french onion soup

Yield: 4 servings

Prep Time: 15 minutes

Cook Time: 1 hour 15 minutes

Before I went vegan, French onion soup was one of my favorite things to order at a restaurant. There is something so amazing about the sweet onions, the bread that soaks up the flavorful broth, and the bubbly cheese on top. I never realized how easy it is to make this soup at home! Even with the vegan substitutes, this version tastes just as good as the original and is great for cold nights. Stale bread works better here, but fresh bread is fine, too.

4 onions, preferably Vidalia (about 2¼ pounds/1kg), thinly sliced

3 tablespoons vegan butter

1 tablespoon olive oil

1 tablespoon organic granulated sugar

½ to ¾ teaspoon salt, divided

1 tablespoon balsamic vinegar

1 quart (950ml) low-sodium vegetable broth

2 bay leaves

Leaves from 3 sprigs fresh thyme, plus more for garnish

8 (½-inch/13mm) slices baguette (preferably stale)

4 slices vegan cheddar cheese

¼ cup (28g) shredded or grated vegan parmesan

1. Caramelize the onions: Place the onions, vegan butter, oil, sugar, and ¼ teaspoon of the salt in a large heavy soup pot. Cook over low heat, stirring occasionally with a wooden spoon, for 45 minutes. The onions will be pale in color and reduced in size. Increase the heat to high and continue to cook uncovered for 25 minutes, stirring frequently. When done, the caramelized onions will be dark brown and extremely soft, and they will almost have formed a paste.

2. In the last 5 minutes of caramelizing the onions, preheat the oven to 350°F (176°C).

3. Lower the heat under the onions to medium. Pour in the balsamic vinegar and stir to deglaze the pan, scraping with the wooden spoon to release anything that is stuck to the bottom.

4. Stir in the broth, bay leaves, and thyme. Simmer over low heat for 15 to 20 minutes to allow the flavors to develop. Taste the soup and add another ¼ teaspoon to ½ teaspoon salt to taste.

5. While the soup simmers, place the slices of bread on a rimmed baking sheet and toast in the preheated oven for 10 minutes, until golden.

6. Remove the bay leaves from the soup and turn the oven to broil on high.

7. Set 4 oven-safe soup bowls on the rimmed baking sheet and divide the soup among the bowls. Place 2 pieces of toasted bread in each bowl. Top with a slice of vegan cheddar and sprinkle the vegan parmesan over the top. Broil for 5 to 10 minutes, until the vegan cheese is melted and the top is bubbly.

8. Garnish with extra thyme and serve warm.

scallion pancakes

Yield: 10 pancakes (8 to 10 servings)

Prep Time: 40 minutes, plus time for dough to rest

Cook Time: 40 minutes

Cong you bing are crispy, flaky Chinese scallion pancakes that are a fun appetizer. They are made from simple ingredients and are easy to prepare. The taste of the green onions is mild; however, if you like a lot of green onion flavor, feel free to add more. These pancakes are a bit lighter than traditional scallion pancakes because less oil is used for frying. Don't worry, though; they're still comforting and delicious.

3½ to 3¾ cups (420g to 450g) all-purpose flour, plus more for dusting

½ teaspoon salt

⅔ cup (160ml) nondairy milk

2 large bunches green onions, thinly sliced (about 2 cups/100g)

5 tablespoons (75g) vegetable oil, divided

DIPPING SAUCE

2 tablespoons low-sodium soy sauce

1 tablespoon maple syrup

1 tablespoon sesame seeds, for garnish

1. Prepare the pancakes: Put the flour, salt, and 1¼ cups (300ml) of hot water in a large bowl. Use a rubber spatula to mix until a shaggy dough forms, then knead the dough with your hands until it forms a rough ball. Dump the dough out onto a clean surface and knead until smooth. It will be slightly tacky but not sticky, and it should be easy to handle. If the dough sticks to your hands as you knead it, add ¼ cup (30g) more flour; if it's too dry, add another 1 tablespoon of water. Wrap in plastic wrap and let rest on the counter for 1 hour.

2. Remove the dough from the plastic wrap and roll it into a log about 20 inches (50cm) long and 1 inch (2.5cm) thick. Cut the dough into 10 equal pieces, each about 2 inches (5cm) long.

3. Cover all but one piece of dough with a clean kitchen towel so they don't dry out. Place the remaining piece on a clean work surface and use a rolling pin to roll the dough as thinly as possible into a square. The dough should not stick to the rolling pin or surface, but if you find it is sticking, lightly dust both the surface and the rolling pin with flour.

4. Use a silicone brush to brush about 1 tablespoon of the nondairy milk over the surface of the dough. Sprinkle about 3 tablespoons of green onions over the dough. Tightly roll up the dough as you would a cinnamon roll; the tighter you roll it, the flakier the pancake will be. Pinch the ends of the rolled-up dough closed and then coil the dough into a spiral. Cover with the towel. Repeat with the remaining dough, milk, and green onions.

5. When you've rolled all of the dough pieces, heat 1½ teaspoons of the oil in a medium-sized nonstick frying pan over medium heat. Use a rolling pin to roll one dough spiral into a pancake about 5 inches (13cm) in diameter and ¼ inch (6mm) thick. If necessary, dust the rolling pin with a small amount of flour to prevent sticking.

6. Place the pancake in the hot oil and cook for about 2 minutes per side, until golden brown and crispy. Transfer to a plate.

7. Repeat Steps 5 and 6 with the remaining dough, using 1½ teaspoons of oil for each pancake. Keep an eye on the pancakes as they cook; if you find they are burning, lower the heat. Stack the finished pancakes on the plate.

8. Meanwhile, prepare the dipping sauce: Put the soy sauce and maple syrup in a small bowl, add 1 tablespoon of water, and mix well.

9. When all of the pancakes are done, slice each circle into quarters and sprinkle with the sesame seeds. Serve immediately with the dipping sauce.

poutine

Yield: 4 servings

Prep Time: 10 minutes
(not including time to make
vegan mozzarella)

Cook Time: 20 minutes

Poutine originated in Québec in the late 1950s. The dish, composed of french fries, gravy, and typically cheese curds, is easy to make. Vegan gravy is just as delicious as regular gravy. In place of cheese curds, vegan mozzarella works perfectly to create an extra layer of creaminess and saltiness.

20 ounces (575g) frozen french fries

GRAVY

3 tablespoons vegan butter

3 tablespoons all-purpose flour

1½ cups (350ml) low-sodium vegetable broth

1 tablespoon low-sodium soy sauce

½ teaspoon garlic powder

¼ teaspoon ground black pepper

Leaves from 2 sprigs fresh thyme, or ¼ teaspoon dried thyme leaves

1 cup (265g) Homemade Vegan Mozzarella (page 190)

FOR GARNISH

Coarse sea salt

Ground black pepper

1 sprig fresh thyme, roughly chopped (optional)

1. Spread out the french fries on a rimmed baking sheet and bake until golden and crispy, according to the package directions.

2. While the fries are baking, prepare the gravy: Melt the vegan butter in a medium-sized saucepan over medium-low heat. Once melted, add the flour and whisk to combine. When the flour is no longer white and is cooked in with the butter, slowly whisk in the broth ¼ cup (60ml) at a time to ensure that the gravy stays smooth. Finally, stir in the remaining ingredients and let the gravy simmer over low heat for 5 minutes, or until thickened.

3. When the fries are done, place them on a large plate. Drizzle the gravy over the top. Add 1- to 2-tablespoon dollops of the vegan mozzarella to the fries to replicate cheese curds. Garnish with coarse salt, pepper, and thyme. Serve warm.

3.

comfort bowls

Bowls have a special place in my heart. They were among the first things I made that became popular on the internet. I had so much fun creating, styling, and photographing them; I was constantly trying new things and evolving my style. The best part about bowls is the endless possibilities. There are so many combinations of ingredients you can put in a bowl, so don't be afraid to get creative.

Vegans have become notorious for loving big bowls of food. These bowls are so satisfying because they incorporate so many elements, flavors, and textures. They also play on different cuisines, which make them all unique in their own way.

This chapter includes recipes made with tofu, chickpeas, homemade seitan, and many other types of plant-based protein. You will find some of my favorite combinations in here, such as the Sesame Tofu Bowl, Thai Red Curry Roasted Cauliflower Bowl, and Fried Tofu with Garlic Mashed Potatoes Bowl. So grab some pretty bowls and get ready to have fun!

creamy balsamic roasted cauliflower bowl

Yield: 2 servings
Prep Time: 20 minutes
Cook Time: 30 minutes

Cauliflower is one of my favorite vegetables. It's so versatile, and it's delicious no matter how you prepare it. In this easy-to-make bowl, roasted cauliflower is coated in a creamy balsamic dressing and paired with farro—an Italian grain that is nutty, similar to brown rice—along with arugula, olives, and cubed vegan mozzarella. Feel free to use a vegan feta instead! Balsamic glaze is just a thickened, sweeter version of balsamic vinegar. You can find it at most grocery stores; I typically get mine from Trader Joe's.

⅔ cup (120g) farro

ROASTED CAULIFLOWER

2 tablespoons cornstarch

1 medium head cauliflower (about 1¼ pounds/570g), cored and cut into florets

CREAMY BALSAMIC SAUCE

2 tablespoons tahini

1½ tablespoons balsamic glaze

1 tablespoon balsamic vinegar

1½ teaspoons olive oil

¼ teaspoon garlic powder

¼ teaspoon onion powder

Salt and pepper, to taste

2 cups (85g) arugula

16 black olives

15 grape tomatoes, halved

3 ounces (85g) vegan mozzarella, cubed

2 teaspoons balsamic glaze, for drizzling

Coarse sea salt, for garnish

1. Preheat the oven to 450°F (232°C). Line a rimmed baking sheet with parchment paper.

2. Cook the farro: In a medium-sized saucepan, bring 3½ cups (830ml) of water to a boil over high heat. While the water comes to boil, rinse the farro. Pour the farro into the boiling water and cook, uncovered, over medium-high heat for 30 minutes. (The farro will be tender but nutty when done, similar to brown rice.)

3. Meanwhile, prepare the cauliflower: Whisk the cornstarch and 1 tablespoon of water in a large bowl; the mixture should be thin. Place the cauliflower florets in the bowl and toss to coat. Transfer the coated cauliflower to the prepared baking sheet and roast for 25 minutes, or until crispy and slightly browned.

4. Meanwhile, prepare the creamy balsamic sauce: In the same large bowl you used for the cauliflower, whisk all of the sauce ingredients with 1 tablespoon of water. The sauce will be thick and creamy but should be easy to pour. If it is too thick, slowly add up to another 1 tablespoon of water until it reaches your desired consistency.

5. Place the roasted cauliflower in the bowl with the sauce and gently toss until all of the florets are coated.

6. Divide the cooked farro, arugula, olives, tomatoes, vegan mozzarella, and roasted cauliflower between serving two bowls. Drizzle 1 teaspoon of the balsamic glaze over each bowl and garnish with coarse salt.

peanut tempeh bowl

Yield: 2 servings

Prep Time: 10 minutes (not including time to cook rice)

Cook Time: 30 minutes

This bowl hits all the right notes—sweet, savory, and nutty. The peanut sauce pairs perfectly with the tempeh. The Brussels sprouts are spicy and a little bit sweet. With fluffy white rice and a pop of color from the red cabbage, this bowl is hearty and satisfying.

PEANUT TEMPEH

1 (8-ounce/224g) package tempeh

3 tablespoons nondairy milk

2 tablespoons all-natural peanut butter

¼ teaspoon Sriracha sauce

1 tablespoon olive oil

SRIRACHA BRUSSELS SPROUTS

14 Brussels sprouts (about 12 ounces/340g), trimmed and halved

1 tablespoon olive oil

2 tablespoons Sriracha sauce

1½ tablespoons maple syrup

½ batch Perfect White Rice (page 191)

1¾ cups (50g) shredded cabbage blend

FOR GARNISH

½ bunch green onions, sliced

1 tablespoon sesame seeds

1. Prepare the tempeh: Use a sharp knife to cut the block of tempeh in half lengthwise. Then make 4 crosswise cuts down the tempeh to form 8 squares. Cut the tempeh squares in half diagonally to make 16 triangles. Place the tempeh in a medium-sized nonstick frying pan with ¼ cup (60ml) of water. Cover and steam over medium heat for 10 minutes.

2. Meanwhile, whisk together the nondairy milk, peanut butter, and Sriracha in a small bowl.

3. When the tempeh is done steaming, uncover and pour the oil over the tempeh. Sauté over medium heat for 7 minutes, flipping every 2 to 3 minutes so that each side gets golden brown. Remove the pan from the heat, pour the sauce over the tempeh, and toss to coat. Reserve about 2 tablespoons of sauce for drizzling over the bowl, if desired.

4. Prepare the Sriracha Brussels sprouts: Place the Brussels sprouts cut side down in a separate medium-sized nonstick frying pan. Pour ½ cup (120ml) of water over them, cover with a lid, and steam over medium-high heat for 10 minutes, until the sprouts darken and soften.

5. Lower the heat to medium. Remove the lid, pour the oil over the Brussels sprouts, and sauté for 10 minutes.

6. Meanwhile, in a small bowl, mix together the Sriracha, maple syrup, and 1 tablespoon of water.

7. When the Brussels sprouts are done, turn the heat to low. Pour the Sriracha maple sauce over the sprouts and cook for 1 to 2 minutes, until the sauce thickens to a glaze.

8. To serve, divide the rice between 2 serving bowls and top with the cabbage, tempeh, and Brussels sprouts. Garnish with the green onions and sesame seeds.

fried tofu with garlic mashed potatoes bowl

Yield: 4 servings

Prep Time: 10 minutes

Cook Time: 35 minutes

This bowl was inspired by Southern cuisine and packs a lot of flavor. The fried tofu is a game changer—it may be the only way you'll want to eat tofu from now on! Combining creamy mashed potatoes, hearty kale, and sweet corn, this bowl is sure to please.

MASHED POTATOES

4 large Yukon Gold potatoes (about 1½ pounds/680g), quartered

10 cloves garlic, peeled

1 teaspoon olive oil

⅓ cup (80ml) nondairy milk

3 tablespoons vegan butter

½ teaspoon salt

FRIED TOFU

1 (16-ounce/454g) block super-firm (high-protein) tofu

3 tablespoons cornstarch

1 teaspoon nutritional yeast

1 teaspoon paprika

½ teaspoon poultry seasoning

½ teaspoon salt

¼ teaspoon ground black pepper

4 tablespoons vegetable or canola oil, divided

4 cups destemmed and chopped raw kale (about 9½ ounces/270g)

2 cloves roasted garlic (from above)

1½ teaspoons olive oil

Pinch of salt

Pinch of red pepper flakes

1 (10-ounce/283g) package frozen corn

1 tablespoon vegan butter

1. Preheat the oven to 400°F (204°C).

2. Start the mashed potatoes: Fill a large saucepan halfway with water. Add the quartered potatoes and boil for 20 minutes, or until fork-tender.

3. Meanwhile, place the garlic cloves in a small baking dish and drizzle the olive oil on top. Toss to coat, then place the dish in the oven and roast the garlic until golden, about 10 minutes.

4. While the potatoes and garlic are cooking, prepare the tofu: Cut the block of tofu in half laterally (working parallel to the cutting board) so you have two thin rectangles. Cut each rectangle lengthwise into 4 long pieces. Cut each of the 8 long pieces in half on the diagonal to create a total of 16 tofu triangles.

5. Put the cornstarch, nutritional yeast, paprika, poultry seasoning, salt, and pepper in a medium-sized bowl and mix together. Take a piece of tofu and dip it in the seasoned cornstarch, coating it completely. Repeat with the remaining pieces of tofu. If there is leftover coating, keep dipping the tofu until all of the coating is used.

6. Pour 2 tablespoons of the vegetable oil into a large frying pan. Allow the oil to warm up over medium heat for 1 minute, then add half of the tofu and cook for 5 minutes, or until golden brown on one side. The oil will be bubbling. Flip the pieces over and cook for 5 minutes on the other side. When the tofu is done, place it on a paper towel–lined dish to drain. Repeat with the remaining oil and tofu.

7. When the potatoes are done, drain any remaining liquid. Add 8 cloves of the roasted garlic, the nondairy milk, vegan butter, and salt to the pan. Using a potato masher or the back of a fork, mash the potatoes until smooth. If needed, add more salt to taste.

 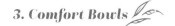

8. Put the kale and ¼ cup (60ml) of water in a large nonstick frying pan over medium heat. Cover with a lid and steam for 6 minutes, or until the kale is bright green and tender. Meanwhile, chop the 2 remaining roasted garlic cloves.

9. Drain any remaining liquid from the kale, then add the olive oil, salt, red pepper flakes, and chopped garlic to the pan. Toss the kale and cook for 4 minutes, or until it has turned slightly darker and a little bit crispy.

10. In a small saucepan, warm the corn and vegan butter over medium heat, stirring until the butter has melted, about 3 minutes. If you prefer your corn slightly browned and crispy, let it cook for 5 to 6 minutes.

11. To serve, scoop the mashed potatoes into bowls and top with the kale, corn, and tofu.

sesame tofu bowl

Yield: 4 servings

Prep Time: 12 minutes (not including time to cook rice)

Cook Time: 25 minutes

This popular recipe from my blog is an easy vegan version of everyone's favorite takeout dish. Crispy pieces of tofu are coated in a sweet and savory sauce and served over a giant scoop of white rice.

TOFU

1 (16-ounce/454g) block extra-firm tofu

3 tablespoons cornstarch

½ teaspoon paprika

Dash of salt

2 tablespoons vegetable or canola oil

SESAME SAUCE

1 tablespoon cornstarch

2 cloves garlic, minced

1 (1-inch/2.5cm) piece ginger, peeled and minced

¼ cup (60ml) low-sodium soy sauce

1½ tablespoons toasted sesame oil

1 tablespoon rice vinegar

¼ cup (50g) packed organic dark brown sugar

2 tablespoons sesame seeds

Pinch of red pepper flakes

1 batch Perfect White Rice (page 191), for serving

FOR GARNISH

1 bunch green onions, chopped

1 tablespoon sesame seeds

1. Prepare the tofu: Remove the tofu from the package and drain the liquid. Wrap the tofu in a clean kitchen towel and press with your hands to remove the excess water.

2. Using a sharp knife, cut the block of tofu in half lengthwise, then turn your knife 90 degrees to cut the two long pieces in half crosswise, making 4 equal-sized rectangles. Cut each rectangle crosswise into 4 pieces, making a total of 16 pieces. Take one piece and cut it in half lengthwise, then cut the 2 long pieces in half crosswise. Repeat with the remaining 15 pieces to make a total of 64 pieces.

3. Put the cornstarch, paprika, and salt in a bowl and mix together. Add the tofu and gently toss to coat. It should absorb the cornstarch and appear wet.

4. Heat the vegetable oil in a large nonstick frying pan over medium heat. Place the tofu in the pan and cook for 3 to 4 minutes per side, until the tofu is golden and a crust has formed.

5. Meanwhile, make the sauce: Start by making a slurry. Put the cornstarch and 1 tablespoon of water in a small bowl and whisk until smooth. It should resemble milk. Place the remaining sauce ingredients along with ½ cup (120ml) of water in a 1-cup (240ml) liquid measuring cup, then add the slurry and whisk to combine. The sauce will look cloudy and light brown.

6. Pour the sauce into a medium-sized saucepan and cook over medium-low heat for about 5 minutes, until it thickens and starts to turn translucent.

7. When the tofu is done, reduce the heat under the frying pan to low. Pour the sauce over the tofu and toss to coat. Cook for an additional 2 minutes to allow the tofu to soak up some of the flavorful sauce.

8. Serve the tofu and sauce immediately with the rice. Garnish with the green onions and sesame seeds.

nourish bowl

Yield: 2 servings

Prep Time: 20 minutes (not including time to soak cashews)

Cook Time: 25 minutes

A bowl filled with veggies may seem boring to some, but this bowl is sure to change your mind. Crispy chickpeas and roasted broccoli pair perfectly with fluffy quinoa, and a drizzle of creamy cashew sauce ties it all together. This bowl is sure to get even the pickiest eater to love veggies.

CRISPY CHICKPEAS

1 (15½-ounce/439g) can chickpeas, drained and rinsed

3 tablespoons barbecue sauce

1½ teaspoons olive oil

½ teaspoon garlic powder

½ teaspoon paprika

ROASTED BROCCOLI

1 large head broccoli (about 12 ounces/340g), cut into florets

1½ teaspoons olive oil

½ teaspoon garlic powder

½ teaspoon onion powder

¼ teaspoon salt

¾ cup (125g) quinoa

CREAMY CASHEW SAUCE

½ cup (60g) cashews, soaked in water overnight

⅓ cup (80ml) nondairy milk, plus more if needed

1 tablespoon maple syrup

1 teaspoon Sriracha sauce

1 clove garlic, peeled

¼ teaspoon salt

1 cup (170g) frozen shelled edamame

½ Hass avocado, sliced

½ cucumber, peeled into ribbons or thinly sliced

1. Place one oven rack in the top third of the oven and a second rack in the lower third. Preheat the oven to 425°F (218°C). Line two large rimmed baking sheets with parchment paper.

2. Prepare the crispy chickpeas: Put the chickpeas, barbecue sauce, oil, garlic powder, and paprika in a large bowl and toss to coat. Spread them out on one of the lined baking sheets so there is a little space between the chickpeas. Roast on the top rack in the oven for 25 minutes, or until crispy and golden.

3. Prepare the roasted broccoli: Put the broccoli in another large bowl and top with the oil, garlic powder, onion powder, and salt. Toss to coat. Spread the broccoli on the second lined baking sheet. Roast on the lower rack in the oven for 15 minutes, or until tender and slightly browned.

4. While the chickpeas and broccoli are in the oven, cook the quinoa: Put the quinoa, 1½ cups (350ml) of water, and a dash of salt in a medium-sized saucepan. Bring to a boil, then cover and simmer for 15 minutes. When done, fluff the quinoa with a fork.

5. Meanwhile, make the cashew sauce: In a high-powered blender, blend the soaked cashews, nondairy milk, maple syrup, Sriracha, garlic, and salt until creamy. If the sauce is not smooth, add 1 to 2 tablespoons more nondairy milk and continue blending until it reaches a smooth consistency.

6. Warm the edamame in a small frying pan with 1 tablespoon of water.

7. To serve, divide the quinoa between 2 bowls. Top with the chickpeas, broccoli, avocado slices, cucumber ribbons, and edamame and drizzle the cashew sauce over the top.

SPECIAL EQUIPMENT:
High-powered blender

pad thai bowl

Yield: 2 servings
Prep Time: 10 minutes
Cook Time: 15 minutes

When I tried pad Thai for the first time, I instantly fell in love. It had so much texture and flavor—it was just delicious. Traditionally, pad Thai is made with fish sauce, but soy sauce replaces it well in this recipe. Pad Thai also includes tamarind paste, which gives the sauce a unique sour flavor. You can find it online or at an Asian market. This bowl is easy and quick to prepare, making it a fun meal to try! Note that the whole chilies in the photo are just for show. Throw some on top as a decoration if you like, but I don't advise eating them!

PAD THAI SAUCE

3 tablespoons low-sodium soy sauce

2 tablespoons organic dark brown sugar

2 tablespoons tamarind paste

3 Thai chilies, chopped, or 1 scant teaspoon red pepper flakes, plus more if desired

Juice of ½ lime

8 ounces (225g) pad Thai rice noodles

2 tablespoons vegetable or canola oil

1 clove garlic, minced

1 large red bell pepper (about 7 ounces/200g), sliced

8 ounces (225g) extra-firm tofu, drained and pressed to remove excess water

FOR GARNISH

1 cup (100g) mung bean sprouts

1 bunch green onions, chopped

½ cup (60g) raw peanuts, chopped

½ lime, sliced

1. Prepare the sauce: Put all of the sauce ingredients in a bowl and stir to combine. The sauce will be a little spicy; add more chopped chilies or red pepper flakes to adjust it to your spice preference, if desired.

2. Cook the rice noodles according to the package directions.

3. Meanwhile, heat the oil in a large nonstick frying pan over medium heat. Add the garlic and bell pepper and sauté for about 5 minutes, until softened.

4. Cut the tofu into thin slices. Add the tofu to the pan with the garlic and bell pepper and cook for 3 minutes, until slightly crispy, then flip and cook until slightly crispy on the other side.

5. When the noodles are cooked, add them to the pan along with the sauce. Cook over low heat for 5 minutes to thicken the sauce.

6. To serve, divide the pad Thai between 2 bowls. Top with the soybean sprouts, green onions, peanuts, and lime slices.

"beef" bulgogi bowl

Yield: 4 servings

Prep Time: 20 minutes, plus time to marinate seitan (not including time to cook rice)

Cook Time: 45 minutes

Bulgogi ("fire meat") is a popular Korean dish consisting of beef that's infused with a sweet, spicy, and savory marinade and then grilled. Homemade seitan makes a great replacement for beef, as it mimics the texture well and soaks up the delicious marinade. Bulgogi pairs wonderfully with rice, fresh vegetables, and kimchi.

SEITAN

2 tablespoons tomato paste

1 tablespoon low-sodium soy sauce

1 cup (120g) vital wheat gluten

¼ cup (30g) chickpea flour

1 teaspoon garlic powder

1 teaspoon onion powder

2½ cups (600ml) low-sodium vegetable broth, divided

MARINADE

½ cup (120ml) pear juice

2 tablespoons low-sodium soy sauce

1 tablespoon gochujang paste

1 tablespoon toasted sesame oil

1 tablespoon organic granulated sugar

6 cloves garlic, minced

2 green onions, chopped

12 heads baby bok choy (about 12½ ounces/355g)

1 batch Perfect White Rice (page 191)

4 green onions, chopped

1 tablespoon toasted sesame oil

1 large cucumber (about 10½ ounces/300g), julienned

4 large carrots (about 8½ ounces/240g), peeled into ribbons or julienned

½ cup (112g) vegan kimchi

1 tablespoon sesame seeds, for garnish

1. Prepare the seitan: Mix together the tomato paste and soy sauce in a medium-sized bowl. Add the vital wheat gluten, chickpea flour, garlic powder, and onion powder and mix with a fork. The mixture will be clumpy. Slowly pour ½ cup (120ml) of the broth into the seitan. Stir to combine. Knead the seitan with your hands for 2 to 3 minutes, or until it bounces back when you touch it.

2. Bring the remaining 2 cups (475ml) of broth and 4 cups (1L) of water to a boil in a sauté pan.

3. On a clean work surface, roll out the seitan with a rolling pin into a large cutlet about ¼ inch (6mm) thick. Carefully transfer the seitan cutlet to the pan and boil over medium heat, uncovered, for 30 minutes. When done, the seitan will have absorbed some of the broth and will look thicker.

4. Meanwhile, prepare the marinade: Place all of the ingredients in a large resealable plastic bag. Seal the bag and squeeze to make sure everything is mixed together.

5. Remove the seitan from the pan and let it cool for 5 minutes, then slice it into thirty-two ¼-inch (6mm) strips. Place the strips in the marinade, seal the bag, and refrigerate for at least 30 minutes or overnight.

6. To finish the seitan, preheat a lightly oiled grill pan or a small portable grill to medium heat. Remove the seitan from the bag (reserving the marinade) and grill it for 2 to 3 minutes per side, or until the seitan has grill marks and is browned and crispy. You will need to do this in 2 or 3 batches.

7. Meanwhile, steam the baby bok choy in a large frying pan with ¼ cup (60ml) of water. When done, drain any excess water and add the leftover seitan marinade. Cook over medium heat for about 4 minutes to thicken the sauce.

8. To the cooked rice, add the green onions and sesame oil. Mix together.

9. To serve, divide the rice among 4 bowls, then add the seitan, bok choy, cucumber, carrots, and kimchi. Garnish with the sesame seeds.

Kimchi is a salty and spicy Korean side dish that is made from fermented cabbage and other vegetables. You can find kimchi at most grocery stores. Be sure to check the ingredients, as some brands contain fish or shrimp paste. You can also make it at home if you prefer.

thai red curry roasted cauliflower bowl

Yield: 4 servings
Prep Time: 12 minutes
Cook Time: 45 minutes

Making a curry can seem overwhelming, but this bowl keeps it simple. Thai red curry paste is easy to find at most grocery stores and Asian markets. The spicy, savory flavor of the paste pairs nicely with the creaminess of the coconut milk. I prefer light coconut milk, but feel free to use full-fat coconut milk if you like—either one will give you a creamy curry. Combined with vegetables, tofu, and brown rice, this bowl is full of comfort and flavor.

1 cup (180g) brown rice

ROASTED CAULIFLOWER

1 large head cauliflower (about 28 ounces/795g), cut into florets

1 tablespoon olive oil

Dash of salt

Dash of ground black pepper

THAI RED CURRY

2 (13½-ounce/400ml) cans coconut milk

2 tablespoons Thai red curry paste, plus more if desired

2 cloves garlic, minced

2 cups (300g) fresh string beans, cut in half

Juice of ½ lime

2 tablespoons maple syrup

4 cups (170g) fresh spinach

TOFU

1 tablespoon toasted sesame oil

1 (16-ounce/454g) block extra-firm tofu

1 tablespoon low-sodium soy sauce

FOR GARNISH

1 tablespoon sesame seeds

½ lime, sliced

1. Place an oven rack in the top position. Preheat the oven to 425°F (218°C). Line a rimmed baking sheet with parchment paper.

2. In a medium-sized saucepan, combine the brown rice and 1¾ cups (415ml) of water. Bring to a boil, then simmer, covered, for 45 minutes, or until soft. When done, fluff the rice with a fork.

3. Meanwhile, place the cauliflower florets in a large bowl. Add the olive oil, salt, and pepper and toss to coat. Spread out the cauliflower on the lined baking sheet. Roast on the top rack in the oven for 20 minutes, or until tender and slightly browned.

4. While the rice and cauliflower are cooking, make the curry: Combine the coconut milk, curry paste, and garlic in a large, deep frying pan. Cook over low heat for 2 to 3 minutes, until the curry paste has dissolved. If you prefer a spicier curry, add more curry paste.

5. Add the string beans, lime juice, and maple syrup to the coconut milk mixture. Cook, stirring occasionally with a rubber spatula, for 7 minutes, or until the beans have softened and the curry has begun to thicken.

6. When the cauliflower is done, add it to the curry along with the spinach. Cook for 1 minute, until the spinach begins to wilt, using the spatula to mix it in. Cover with a lid until ready to serve.

7. Prepare the tofu: Remove the tofu from the package and drain the liquid. Wrap the tofu in a clean kitchen towel and press with your hands to remove the excess water. Cut the block of tofu into quarters. Cut each quarter into 4 rectangular slices, then cut each slice into 4 equal-sized cubes. This will give you 64 cubes.

Thai red curry paste is a paste made from red bell pepper, red chilies, garlic, ginger, and shallot. It is typically sold in a small jar. You need only a little bit, as it is spicy!

8.   Pour the sesame oil into a large nonstick frying pan over medium heat, then add the tofu cubes. Pan-fry for 3 to 4 minutes, until golden. (If your frying pan is smaller, fry the tofu cubes in 2 batches to avoid overcrowding them.) Flip the tofu cubes and cook for 3 to 4 minutes on another side. Add the soy sauce and cook for another 1 to 2 minutes, until the tofu absorbs the sauce and turns crispy again.

9.   To serve, place a scoop of rice in each of 4 bowls and top with the curry and crispy tofu. Sprinkle with the sesame seeds and garnish with 1 or 2 lime slices.

southwestern polenta bowl

Yield: 2 servings
Prep Time: 10 minutes
Cook Time: 30 minutes

Creamy polenta paired with spiced black beans is a perfect combination. Polenta is simply an Italian boiled cornmeal, and it can be served in a variety of ways. In this dish, the polenta is warm and creamy, similar to porridge. To make it even creamier, stir an additional ¼ cup (60ml) of nondairy milk into the cooled polenta before scooping it into the bowls.

CREAMY POLENTA

1 cup (140g) polenta

2 cups (475ml) low-sodium vegetable broth

1 cup (240ml) nondairy milk

¼ teaspoon salt

1 tablespoon vegan butter

SOUTHWESTERN BLACK BEANS

1 tablespoon olive oil

½ large red bell pepper (about 3½ ounces/100g), chopped

¼ small red onion, chopped

1 (4-ounce/113g) can hatch chilies, with liquid

1 (15½-ounce/439g) can black beans, drained

1 teaspoon paprika

1 teaspoon chili powder

½ teaspoon ground cumin

¼ cup (60ml) low-sodium vegetable broth

Salt and pepper

1 cup (135g) frozen corn

FOR GARNISH

½ Hass avocado, sliced

2 to 4 jalapeño peppers, depending on spice tolerance, sliced

1 lime, sliced

1. Make the creamy polenta: Put the polenta, broth, nondairy milk, and salt in a 2-quart saucepan. Cook over medium-low heat, whisking occasionally to prevent clumping, for 10 minutes. The polenta will start to thicken. After 10 minutes, reduce the heat to a low simmer, cover with a lid, and cook for another 20 minutes, or until the polenta is very thick and soft, with no grittiness.

2. While the polenta is cooking, make the Southwestern black beans: Place the oil, bell pepper, onion, and chilies with their liquid in a large nonstick frying pan over medium heat. Cook for 5 minutes, or until the bell pepper has softened and the onion is starting to turn translucent.

3. Add the beans, spices, and broth, reduce the heat to low, and cook for another 7 to 8 minutes, until everything is softened and warm. Using a rubber spatula, lightly crush some of the black beans to make a sort of paste. Before serving, season the beans with salt and pepper to taste.

4. Put the corn in a medium-sized nonstick frying pan over medium heat with 1 to 2 tablespoons of water. Simmer the corn for 3 to 4 minutes, until it is fully warmed.

5. When the polenta is done, remove it from the heat and stir in the vegan butter.

6. To serve, divide the polenta, beans, and corn between 2 bowls. Garnish with the avocado, jalapeño, and lime slices.

bang bang tofu bowl

Yield: 2 servings
Prep Time: 12 minutes
Cook Time: 30 minutes

The stars of this bowl are cubes of panko-crusted tofu coated in sweet, creamy, and spicy Bang Bang sauce, which is simple to make and extremely delicious. For the noodles, use fresh ramen or yakisoba noodles, which can be found at Asian markets or larger grocery stores. If you can't find them, you can always use a dry noodle (see note, opposite). Pairing flavorful tofu and noodles with edamame and cucumber, this bowl really packs a punch.

CRISPY TOFU

8 ounces (225g) extra-firm tofu, drained and pressed to remove excess water

⅓ cup (18g) panko breadcrumbs

BANG BANG SAUCE

2½ tablespoons vegan mayonnaise

2 tablespoons sweet chili sauce

2 teaspoons Sriracha sauce

SOY GARLIC NOODLES

2 cloves garlic, chopped

1 tablespoon toasted sesame oil

6 ounces (170g) fresh ramen or yakisoba noodles

1 tablespoon low-sodium soy sauce

4 cups (400g) frozen shelled edamame

½ cucumber, halved lengthwise and then sliced into half-moons

2 green onions, sliced on a bias, for garnish

Black and white sesame seeds, for garnish

1. Preheat the oven to 450°F (232°C). Line a rimmed baking sheet with parchment paper.

2. Using a sharp knife, cut the tofu in half. Cut each half into 4 rectangular slices, then cut each slice into 4 equal-sized cubes. This will give you 32 cubes.

3. Put the panko in a bowl, add the tofu, and toss to coat. Because the tofu is wet, the breadcrumbs will easily stick.

4. Place the tofu on the prepared baking sheet. Bake for 25 minutes, flipping the cubes over in the last 5 minutes of cooking. They should be golden.

5. Meanwhile, prepare the Bang Bang sauce: Mix together the vegan mayonnaise, sweet chili sauce, and Sriracha in a medium-sized bowl.

6. Prepare the noodles: In a medium-sized nonstick frying pan, cook the garlic in the sesame oil over low heat, stirring frequently, for 2 minutes. When the garlic is fragrant, add the noodles and soy sauce. Cook for 3 minutes to warm the noodles.

7. Put the edamame in a large frying pan with 2 tablespoons of water. Cover and steam over medium heat for 5 minutes, until warmed.

8. When the tofu is done, place it in the bowl with the sauce and toss to coat.

9. To serve, arrange the tofu, noodles, edamame, and cucumber slices in 2 bowls. Garnish with the green onions and sesame seeds.

If using dry noodles, cook them according to the package directions. Drain and add the cooked noodles to the pan with the garlic as directed in Step 6.

4.

mains

Having reliable recipes that you can make for yourself and for others is so important. This chapter explores all kinds of main dishes, from soups and sandwiches to pasta and pizza and more. All of these recipes will work perfectly as a main dish for your family or for a dinner party—or for yourself, and then you'll have leftovers.

This chapter includes some of my favorite family recipes, such as Escarole and Beans, Meaty Vegan Lasagna, and Homemade Manicotti. You'll also find vegan versions of classic American comfort dishes such as Chick'n and Dumplings, Meaty Vegan Burgers, and Vegan Mac and Cheese. All of the recipes in this chapter are designed to serve four or more people, so be sure to keep that in mind. All of these meals would pair great with a side salad or some vegetables of choice. Now, grab a pan and let's get cooking!

broccoli and cheddar twice-baked potatoes

Yield: 4 servings

Prep Time: 15 minutes, plus time to soak cashews (not including time to make tempeh bacon)

Cook Time: 1 hour 10 minutes

Twice-baked potatoes are pure comfort. You take a baked potato, scoop out the insides and mash them with the filling ingredients of your choice, and then stuff the potato with the mixture. Combining the saltiness of tempeh bacon, the creaminess of cheddar cheese sauce, and the brightness of broccoli, this version has it all. You'll need a high-powered blender for this recipe to get a smooth cheese sauce.

4 russet potatoes (about 3 pounds/1.4kg)

1 broccoli crown (about 5½ ounces/155g), cut into florets

¼ cup (60ml) nondairy milk

3 tablespoons vegan butter

1 batch Tempeh Bacon Crumbles (page 186)

Salt

CHEDDAR CHEESE SAUCE

1 cup (120g) raw cashews, soaked in water overnight, rinsed, and drained

⅔ cup (160ml) nondairy milk

½ carrot (about ½ ounce/15g), peeled

1½ teaspoons nutritional yeast

½ teaspoon salt

Pinch of ground black pepper

Pinch of turmeric powder

SPECIAL EQUIPMENT: High-powered blender

If you have leftover cheese sauce, store it in the refrigerator for up to 4 days.

1. Preheat the oven to 450°F (232°C).

2. Pierce the potatoes with a fork and bake directly on the oven rack for 1 hour, or until soft.

3. Meanwhile, prepare the cheese sauce: Put all of the ingredients for the sauce in a high-powered blender and blend until very smooth. Adjust the seasonings to taste.

4. Bring ½ cup (120ml) of water to a boil in a large saucepan. Put the broccoli in the pan, cover with a lid, and steam over medium heat for 5 minutes, or until bright green. Drain, let cool for 5 minutes, and then finely chop the broccoli.

5. When the potatoes are done, remove them from the oven and reduce the oven temperature to 350°F (176°C). Allow the potatoes to cool for 5 minutes before handling.

6. Slice the top third off of each potato and place the tops in a large bowl. Scrape out the insides, leaving just a shell, and place the insides in the bowl with the tops.

7. Using a potato masher, mash the potato tops and insides with the nondairy milk, vegan butter, and ¼ cup (80g) of the cheese sauce. The mashed potatoes should be very smooth.

8. Fold three-quarters of the broccoli and three-quarters of the tempeh bacon crumbles into the mashed potatoes, reserving the remainder for topping. Season with salt to taste.

9. Divide the mashed potato mixture among the 4 potato shells, filling them to the top. Top with the reserved broccoli and tempeh bacon crumbles, then drizzle with the cheese sauce. (You will likely have some sauce left over.)

10. Bake the stuffed potatoes for 10 minutes, until warmed through and a bit crispy on top. Serve immediately with any remaining cheese sauce.

buffalo chick'n sandwiches

Yield: 4 sandwiches
Prep Time: 15 minutes
Cook Time: 1 hour

Homemade seitan and Buffalo sauce are a match made in heaven. Buffalo sauce is a tangy, vinegary, salty hot sauce that originated in Buffalo, New York. Don't worry, it isn't made from buffalo; however, some brands of Buffalo sauce do contain dairy, so be sure to check the ingredients. This recipe combines many flavors and textures to make a truly delicious sandwich.

SEITAN

½ cup (120g) canned chickpeas, drained and rinsed

1½ teaspoons Buffalo sauce

1 cup (120g) vital wheat gluten

1 tablespoon poultry seasoning

1½ teaspoons garlic powder

1½ teaspoons onion powder

Pinch of salt

Pinch of ground black pepper

2½ cups (600ml) low-sodium vegetable broth, divided

BATTER

½ cup (60g) chickpea flour

BREADING

1 cup (160g) fine breadcrumbs

1 tablespoon paprika

2 teaspoons garlic powder

2 teaspoons onion powder

¾ cup (180ml) Buffalo sauce

¼ cup (60ml) nondairy milk

½ cup (104g) vegan mayonnaise

4 sandwich rolls of choice

½ cup (30g) shredded lettuce

½ medium cucumber (about 3 ounces/85g), thinly sliced

1. Prepare the seitan: Put the chickpeas and Buffalo sauce in a large bowl and mash with a fork. Add the vital wheat gluten and seasonings and mix with the fork until large crumbles form. Pour in ½ cup (120ml) of the broth and continue to mix; the seitan will absorb the liquid. Knead with your hands for 5 minutes, until the seitan comes together. It should be spongy and springy.

2. Bring the remaining 2 cups (475ml) of broth and 4 cups (950ml) of water to a boil in a medium-sized pot. Divide the seitan into 4 equal pieces and, using a rolling pin, roll them into oval shapes, about ½ inch (13mm) thick. Boil the seitan for 30 minutes, until most of the liquid is absorbed and the seitan is puffy and has increased in size.

3. Meanwhile, prepare the batter: Whisk together the chickpea flour and 1 cup (240ml) of water in a medium-sized bowl.

4. Prepare the breading: Mix together the breadcrumbs and seasonings on a large flat plate.

5. When the seitan is done, drain any excess liquid. Allow to cool for 5 minutes; the seitan will be very hot.

6. Preheat the oven to 400°F (204°C). Line a rimmed baking sheet with parchment paper.

7. Dip a piece of seitan into the batter, making sure it is well coated. Allow any excess batter to drip back into the bowl. Roll the battered seitan in seasoned breadcrumbs, breading each side very well. Place on the prepared baking sheet. Repeat with the remaining seitan, batter, and breadcrumbs.

8. Bake the seitan for 20 minutes. Flip the pieces over, then bake for 10 more minutes, until the outsides are golden and crispy.

9. Meanwhile, make the sauce: Mix together the Buffalo sauce and nondairy milk in a large bowl. When the seitan is done, add the pieces to the bowl and toss to coat them in the sauce.

10. Assemble the sandwiches: Spread 1 tablespoon of vegan mayonnaise on the top half of a roll and 1 tablespoon on the bottom half. Place one-quarter of the shredded lettuce on the bottom half, then add a piece of seitan and a few cucumber slices. Repeat with the remaining ingredients to make 4 sandwiches.

meaty vegan lasagna

Yield: 8 servings

Prep Time: 20 minutes
(not including time to make
tomato sauce or tofu ricotta)

Cook Time: 1 hour

If you have never made a vegan lasagna, I promise this recipe is about to blow your mind. It is just as good as, if not better than, regular meat-and-cheese lasagna. Just like with any lasagna, this recipe involves a few steps, but the end result is so worth it. If you prefer a saucier lasagna, prepare a little extra tomato sauce (see note, opposite).

1 (14-ounce/400g) package vegan ground beef

1½ teaspoons olive oil

1 batch Tomato Sauce (page 189)

16 lasagna noodles (12 ounces/ 340g)

1 batch Tofu Ricotta (page 188)

1½ cups (168g) vegan mozzarella shreds

Leaves from 3 sprigs fresh parsley, chopped, for garnish

1.   Preheat the oven to 450°F (232°C).

2.   In a large frying pan, sauté the vegan ground beef in the oil over medium heat for 5 minutes, until slightly crispy and warmed through. Add the tomato sauce and simmer over very low heat for 10 minutes, stirring occasionally.

3.   Meanwhile, bring a large pot of salted water to a boil over high heat. Add the lasagna noodles and boil until slightly undercooked, or 1 to 2 minutes less than the suggested cooking time on the package. (You want to undercook them slightly because they will continue to cook in the oven.) Drain the noodles but leave a little bit of water in the pot so they don't stick together.

4.   To assemble the lasagna, layer the ingredients as follows:

Layer 1: Spread ½ cup (140g) of the "meat" sauce across the bottom of a 9 by 13-inch (23 by 33cm) baking dish. Lay 4 lasagna noodles across the bottom of the pan; depending on the size of the noodles, you may need to cut them to fit. Spread ½ cup (110g) of the tofu ricotta over the noodles with a spatula. Sprinkle ½ cup (56g) of the vegan mozzarella shreds evenly over the ricotta.

Layer 2: Spread 1 cup (280g) of the sauce over the vegan cheeses. Layer 4 lasagna noodles lengthwise over the sauce. Then spread ½ cup (110g) of the tofu ricotta over the noodles and sprinkle with ½ cup (56g) of the mozzarella shreds.

Layer 3: Repeat layer 2, but without the mozzarella shreds, then spread 1 cup (280g) of sauce over the ricotta.

Layer 4: Layer the final 4 lasagna noodles over the sauce. Spread the remaining ricotta and sauce over the noodles, then top with the remaining mozzarella shreds.

If you prefer your lasagna saucier, prepare 1½ batches of tomato sauce.

5. Cover with aluminum foil and bake for 40 minutes. Remove the foil and bake uncovered for 5 minutes to allow the vegan cheese on top to become slightly browned and bubbly. If you like your lasagna crispy, broil on high for 5 minutes.

6. Allow the lasagna to rest for 15 minutes before cutting. Garnish with the parsley and serve.

sheet pan tofu cutlets with roasted vegetables

Yield: 4 servings
Prep Time: 15 minutes
Cook Time: 45 minutes

This meal feels fancy and is perfect for a special occasion, but it's simple to make because the oven does all of the work (which makes it an excellent weeknight dinner, too!). I've included some of my favorite vegetables in this recipe, but you can use any vegetables you like for roasting. The sauce is sweet and tangy and nicely complements the tofu. After you make this once, I know you'll be hooked!

TOFU CUTLETS

1 (16-ounce/454g) block super-firm (high-protein) tofu

2 tablespoons cornstarch

1½ teaspoons nutritional yeast

1 teaspoon garlic powder

1 teaspoon onion powder

½ teaspoon paprika

¼ teaspoon salt

ROASTED VEGETABLES

12 baby Yukon Gold potatoes (about 1¼ pounds/570g), quartered

16 Brussels sprouts (about 1 pound/454g), trimmed and halved

30 rainbow or orange baby carrots (about 12 ounces/340g)

2 tablespoons olive oil

1 teaspoon garlic powder

1 teaspoon onion powder

½ teaspoon dried parsley, plus more for garnish

½ teaspoon paprika

¼ teaspoon ground black pepper

¼ teaspoon salt

SAUCE

2 tablespoons maple syrup

1½ tablespoons low-sodium soy sauce

1 tablespoon ketchup

1 teaspoon apple cider vinegar

½ teaspoon garlic powder

1. Preheat the oven to 425°F (218°C). Line a rimmed baking sheet with parchment paper.

2. Prepare the tofu cutlets: Cut the block of tofu crosswise into 4 equal-sized rectangles. On a large plate, mix the cornstarch, nutritional yeast, spices, and salt. Dip each tofu cutlet in the seasoned cornstarch, coating all sides evenly. Place on the prepared baking sheet, to one side.

3. Prepare the roasted vegetables: Place all of the vegetables in a large bowl, drizzle with the oil, and add the spices and salt. Toss until the vegetables are well coated. Spread the vegetables in a single layer on the other half of the baking sheet, making sure the Brussels sprouts are cut side down.

4. Bake for 25 minutes, then use a spatula to flip over the tofu cutlets. Bake for 10 minutes more.

5. Meanwhile, prepare the sauce: In a medium-sized bowl, mix together all of the ingredients.

6. Remove the baking sheet from the oven and brush the tofu cutlets generously with the sauce, reserving about 2 tablespoons for drizzling later.

7. Return the pan to the oven and bake for another 8 to 10 minutes, until the tofu is crispy, the glaze is thick, and the vegetables are tender.

8. To serve, cut each tofu cutlet crosswise into 5 even pieces and place on a platter with all of the vegetables, or place a whole cutlet on each of 4 plates and evenly divide the vegetables among the plates. Drizzle the reserved sauce over the tofu and garnish with more dried parsley. Season with additional salt and pepper to taste.

deep dish pizza

Yield: two 8-inch (20cm) pizzas (4 servings)

Prep Time: 20 minutes, plus time for dough to rise (not including time to make vegan mozzarella)

Cook Time: 25 minutes

Making homemade pizza is a fun family activity. It's a great way to involve loved ones in cooking, and the end result is always delicious. This deep dish pizza is just as saucy and cheesy as a non-vegan one, so skip the trip to Chicago and make some in your own kitchen right now.

DOUGH

1 (¼-ounce/7g) packet active dry yeast

1 tablespoon organic granulated sugar

3¼ cups (390g) all-purpose flour

½ teaspoon salt

2 tablespoons olive oil, plus more for the bowl and pans

SAUCE

1 (28-ounce/794g) can crushed tomatoes

1 tablespoon organic granulated sugar

½ teaspoon garlic powder

½ teaspoon dried oregano leaves

¼ teaspoon salt

Pinch of red pepper flakes, plus more for topping

1 batch Homemade Vegan Mozzarella (page 190)

2 tablespoons shredded or grated vegan parmesan, divided, for topping

1 teaspoon dried parsley flakes, divided, for topping

1. Prepare the dough: Put the yeast in 1 cup (240ml) of warm water that is between 100°F and 110°F (37°C and 43°C). Add the sugar and set aside to proof for 10 minutes, until foamy.

2. In a large bowl, mix together the flour and salt. Pour the proofed yeast and the oil into the bowl. Mix with a spoon until you have a shaggy dough.

3. Turn the dough out onto a clean, lightly floured surface and knead with your hands for 5 to 10 minutes, until you can form it into a smooth ball. Oil the bowl well, return the dough to the bowl, cover with a clean kitchen towel, and set in a warm, draft-free place, such as a turned-off oven. Allow to rise for 1 hour, or until doubled in size.

4. While the dough is rising, prepare the sauce: In a medium-sized bowl, mix together all of the ingredients. Set aside until ready to use.

5. When the dough has risen, preheat the oven to 475°F (246°C). Generously grease two 8 by 2-inch (20 by 5cm) pie pans or springform pans with oil (or work in batches if you have only one pan).

6. Divide the dough into 2 equal portions. On a clean, lightly floured surface, roll out each portion into a 9-inch (23cm) circle that is ¼ inch (6mm) thick. Drape the dough over the greased pans and use your hands to push it into the pans, working it all the way up the sides to form the deep dish crust.

7. Spread ¾ cup (200g) of the vegan mozzarella over each crust. Spread half of the sauce over the cheese in each pan.

8. Bake the pizzas for 20 minutes, then rotate the pans 180 degrees and bake for 5 more minutes. Remove from the oven and top the pizzas with the vegan parmesan, parsley, and more red pepper flakes. Allow to cool for 10 minutes before cutting, then cut each pizza into 4 or 6 slices.

escarole and beans

Yield: 6 to 8 servings

Prep Time: 10 minutes

Cook Time: 40 minutes

This is one of my favorite meals, and I have to say, no one makes escarole and beans better than my mom. It is an easy dish to make, and the flavors are simple but so incredibly delicious. If you aren't familiar with escarole, it is a big leafy green that belongs to the same family as endive, frisée, and radicchio. Escarole can be dirty, so make sure to wash it very well (see note below). This soup pairs great with hearty bread, and the leftovers can be frozen.

1 vegetable bouillon cube

3 heads escarole (about 3 pounds/1.4kg), thoroughly cleaned and roughly chopped

¼ teaspoon ground black pepper, plus more for garnish

Pinch of salt

6 cloves garlic, sliced

1 tablespoon olive oil

2 (19-ounce/539g) cans cannellini beans, drained and rinsed

¼ teaspoon red pepper flakes, plus more for garnish

1. Pour 4 quarts (3.8L) of water into a 5-quart (4.75L) or larger stockpot, then add the bouillon cube, escarole, pepper, and salt. Cover and bring to a boil over medium-high heat. Continue to boil until the escarole is beginning to wilt, about 20 minutes.

2. In a large frying pan over low heat, cook the garlic in the oil for 5 minutes, until fragrant.

3. Pour the beans into the pan and sprinkle with the red pepper flakes. Increase the heat to medium-low and cook, stirring occasionally, for 10 minutes, until the beans turn slightly golden and soft.

4. When the escarole is starting to wilt, uncover the pot and stir the soup. Boil the escarole, uncovered, for 15 more minutes, or until the escarole is dark green and tender.

5. Pour ½ cup (120ml) of the soup broth into the pan with the beans. Simmer over medium-low heat for 2 to 3 minutes, allowing the beans to absorb the broth.

6. Add the beans to the soup and stir. Season with salt and pepper to taste. Serve immediately garnished with a pinch of black pepper and red pepper flakes.

The best way to clean escarole is to hold the head upside down under the faucet. Then wash every leaf individually, making sure to remove all of the dirt. While this process can be tedious, using escarole that is not properly cleaned will result in a gritty soup. Please do not skip this step!

meaty vegan burgers

Yield: 4 burgers
Prep Time: 20 minutes
Cook Time: 25 minutes

These burgers are meaty, chewy, and full of incredible texture. Combining tempeh and textured vegetable protein creates a vegan burger that is meaty as opposed to veggielike. Of course, there is nothing wrong with a good black bean burger, but sometimes you want something with that classic burger texture. It is best to cook these burgers in a frying pan; do not try to grill them.

BURGERS

4 ounces (115g) tempeh, grated

1 cup (96g) textured vegetable protein (TVP)

1 cup (240ml) low-sodium vegetable broth

2½ tablespoons finely chopped onions (about 1 ounce/28g)

2 cloves garlic, minced

1½ tablespoons olive oil, divided

2 egg replacers (see pages 11–12)

2 tablespoons tomato paste

1 tablespoon low-sodium soy sauce

½ teaspoon garlic powder

½ teaspoon onion powder

¼ teaspoon ground black pepper

BURGER SAUCE

¼ cup (68g) ketchup

3 tablespoons vegan mayonnaise

1 teaspoon maple syrup

1 teaspoon onion powder

Pinch of salt

4 seeded hamburger buns

8 butter lettuce leaves

8 thin slices beefsteak tomato

4 slices vegan cheddar cheese

1. Using the largest holes on a box grater, grate the tempeh into a medium-sized nonstick frying pan. Add 1 cup (240ml) of water, cover, and set over high heat. Steam for 15 minutes, or until all of the water has been absorbed. Remove the lid for the last 3 minutes of steaming.

2. Put the TVP in a medium-sized bowl and pour in the broth. Set aside for 5 minutes, until the TVP has absorbed the liquid.

3. Meanwhile, in a separate medium-sized frying pan, cook the onions and garlic in ½ tablespoon of the oil over medium-low heat for 2 to 3 minutes, until fragrant. Transfer to a large bowl.

4. To the bowl with the onions and garlic, add the steamed tempeh, rehydrated TVP, egg replacers, tomato paste, soy sauce, and seasonings and mix with a fork until well combined.

5. Using a ½-cup (120ml) measuring cup, scoop up a portion of the mixture and form it into a patty about ½ inch (13mm) thick. (If you have a scale, you can weigh a 5-ounce (140g) portion.) Repeat with the rest of the mixture to make 4 patties.

6. Pour the remaining 1 tablespoon of oil into a large nonstick frying pan over medium-low heat. Allow the oil to heat up for 1 minute. Place the burger patties in the pan, increase the heat to medium-high, and cook for 5 minutes per side, or until turning golden brown. If you have to cook them in 2 batches, use ½ tablespoon of oil per batch.

7. Meanwhile, prepare the sauce: Put all of the sauce ingredients in a small bowl and stir until well incorporated. Taste and add more salt if desired.

8. To assemble the burgers, spread 2 tablespoons of burger sauce on the top and bottom half of each bun. Stack a leaf of lettuce, 2 tomato slices, a burger patty, a slice of vegan cheddar, and another lettuce leaf on each bottom half. Top with the top halves of the buns.

yellow split pea cannellini bean stew

Yield: 4 servings

Prep Time: 10 minutes

Cook Time: 1 hour

Cozy up with a bowl of this luscious and comforting stew. Yellow split peas are different from green split peas; they are more tender, have less of an earthy taste, and are closer to red lentils. Combined with coconut milk and cannellini beans, they make this stew a real treat that is sure to satisfy vegans and non-vegans alike.

1 cup (200g) yellow split peas

2 tablespoons olive oil

⅓ onion, preferably Vidalia (about 3 ounces/85g), chopped

4 cloves garlic, minced

1 teaspoon paprika

½ teaspoon chili powder

½ teaspoon red pepper flakes, plus more for garnish if desired

2 (15½-ounce/439g) cans cannellini beans, drained and rinsed

1 (13½-ounce/400ml) can coconut milk

3 cups (710ml) low-sodium vegetable broth

Salt and pepper

3 tablespoons microgreens, for garnish

1. In a medium-sized saucepan, boil the split peas in 3 cups (710ml) of water over medium-high heat for 20 minutes, or until softened.

2. Meanwhile, pour the oil into a medium-sized pot and allow to heat up over medium-low heat for 1 minute.

3. Add the onion and garlic and cook, stirring frequently, for 5 minutes. The onion will start to turn translucent and the garlic will be fragrant. Do not let them burn. If you see anything burning, lower the heat and remove any burnt bits.

4. Sprinkle the paprika, chili powder, and red pepper flakes over the onion and garlic. Allow the spices to warm up for 1 to 2 minutes. Everything will start to appear bright orange.

5. Pour the beans into the pot and continue to cook, stirring often, for 5 minutes. The beans will soften and take on a beautiful orange color from the spices.

6. Drain the split peas and add them to the pot.

7. Reserve ¼ cup (60ml) of the coconut milk for serving. Pour the remaining coconut milk and the broth into the pot.

8. Simmer the stew over low heat, uncovered, for 45 minutes. The stew will thicken and the split peas will become very soft.

9. Lightly crush some of the split peas and beans with a rubber spatula to thicken the stew even more. Season the stew with salt and pepper to taste.

10. Serve in bowls, garnished with a drizzle of the remaining coconut milk, a small bunch of microgreens, and a pinch of red pepper flakes, if desired.

lentil sloppy joes

Yield: 4 sandwiches
Prep Time: 10 minutes
Cook Time: 50 minutes

An easy alternative to traditional sloppy joes, this vegan version uses lentils to replace ground beef. Lentils are little powerhouses of nutrition; they are so good for you and so yummy. I prefer green lentils for this recipe because they hold their shape a bit better than brown lentils, but either type will work great here. To speed up the process, you can skip Step 1 and use precooked brown lentils. Serve these sandwiches with the vegetable of your choice and of course a few kosher dill pickle slices, and you have an easy and delicious meal.

1 cup (200g) green or brown lentils

¼ onion (about 2 ounces/55g), chopped

2 cloves garlic, minced

1 tablespoon olive oil

⅔ cup (180g) ketchup

2 tablespoons low-sodium soy sauce

1 tablespoon prepared yellow mustard

2 tablespoons organic dark brown sugar

1 teaspoon chili powder

1 teaspoon garlic powder

Salt and pepper

4 hamburger buns

1. Boil the lentils in 3 cups (710ml) of water in a medium-sized saucepan over high heat for 45 minutes, or until soft and completely cooked through.

2. When the lentils have 5 minutes of cooking time left, put the garlic, onion, and oil in a medium-sized frying pan over medium heat and sauté for 5 minutes, or until the garlic is fragrant and the onion is translucent.

3. When the lentils are cooked, add them to the pan with the onion and garlic. Add the ketchup, soy sauce, mustard, brown sugar, chili powder, and garlic powder. Use a spatula to mix everything together, then stir in ¼ cup (60ml) of water to make it saucy. Simmer for 5 minutes, until the ingredients are well incorporated. Season with salt and pepper to taste.

4. Meanwhile, toast the buns in a separate nonstick frying pan over medium heat for 2 to 3 minutes, until slightly golden.

5. To serve, divide the lentil mixture evenly among the buns.

homemade manicotti

Yield: 4 to 5 servings

Prep Time: 20 minutes (not including time to make tomato sauce, tofu ricotta, or vegan mozzarella)

Cook Time: 1 hour

Homemade crepe-style manicotti is truly a treat. My family would serve it every year for Christmas. The outside is a very thin crespelle (crepe) that melts in your mouth; it is much more delicate than the pasta tubes that are often used to make manicotti. The crepes in this vegan version are filled with a light, fluffy tofu ricotta and served with gooey melted vegan cheese. Although this dish does require a bit of time and effort to prepare, nothing good comes easy, right?

CRESPELLE

2 cups (240g) all-purpose flour

¼ teaspoon salt

2 egg replacers (see pages 11–12)

1 batch Tomato Sauce (page 189)

1 batch Tofu Ricotta (page 188)

1 batch Homemade Vegan Mozzarella (page 190)

3 tablespoons shredded or grated vegan parmesan

5 fresh basil leaves, chiffonaded

1. Prepare the crespelle: In a large bowl, whisk together the flour and salt. Add the egg replacers and 2⅓ cups (555ml) of water and whisk until a thin, smooth batter forms.

2. Pour about ⅓ cup (70g) of the batter into a 9½-inch (24cm) nonstick frying pan. Cook over low heat for 2 to 3 minutes, until the sides curl up. Flip the crepe and cook for 1 minute on the other side. Repeat with the remaining batter, stacking the cooked crepes on a plate; you will make a total of 10 crepes.

3. Preheat the oven to 350°F (176°C).

4. Pour 1 cup (255g) of the tomato sauce into a 9 by 13-inch (23 by 28cm) baking dish. Spread with a spoon to evenly coat the bottom.

5. Take a crepe and place 2 heaping tablespoons of the tofu ricotta in the bottom half in a log shape. Roll up the crepe and place it seam side down in the baking dish. Repeat until all of the manicotti have been made.

6. Spread ½ cup (128g) of the tomato sauce over the tops of the manicotti. Then spread the vegan mozzarella over the top.

7. Cover with aluminum foil and bake for 20 minutes, then remove the foil and bake uncovered for another 10 minutes, or until the cheese is melted and bubbly and the tops of the manicotti are crispy. Allow to rest for 10 minutes before serving. While it rests, warm the remaining tomato sauce in a small saucepan.

8. To serve, top the manicotti with the vegan parmesan and basil. Serve with the warm tomato sauce.

chick'n marsala

Yield: 4 servings
Prep Time: 15 minutes
Cook Time: 50 minutes

A quick and easy pan sauce made with Marsala cooking wine gives this dish a scrumptious flavor. It is a little bit sweet, filled with onion and garlic and bits of golden, crispy seitan. Most restaurants put mushrooms in their Marsala sauce, but my version is mushroom-free (if you want to add mushrooms, though, see the note, opposite). Pair this dish with pasta, mashed potatoes, or rice for a delicious dinner.

SEITAN

½ cup (130g) canned cannellini beans, drained and rinsed

1 cup (120g) vital wheat gluten

1 teaspoon poultry seasoning

½ teaspoon garlic powder

½ teaspoon onion powder

¼ teaspoon salt

Pinch of ground black pepper

2½ cups (600ml) low-sodium vegetable broth, divided

2 tablespoons vegan butter, plus more for the pan if needed

1 tablespoon olive oil

¼ onion (about 2 ounces/55g), chopped

2 cloves garlic, minced

¾ cup (90g) all-purpose flour

⅔ cup (160ml) Marsala wine

⅔ cup (160ml) low-sodium vegetable broth

1 tablespoon organic granulated sugar, or more to taste

¼ teaspoon salt

¼ teaspoon ground black pepper, plus more for garnish

1 tablespoon cornstarch

A few fresh parsley leaves, for garnish

1. Prepare the seitan: Put the beans in a large bowl and mash with a fork. Add the vital wheat gluten and stir with a spoon. Large clumps will form. Add the seasonings and mix to combine. Slowly pour in ½ cup (120ml) of the broth and mix until the liquid has been absorbed. Knead the seitan with your hands for 1 to 2 minutes, until spongy.

2. In a medium-sized pot, bring the remaining 2 cups (475ml) of broth and 4 cups (950ml) of water to a boil over high heat.

3. Divide the seitan into 4 equal portions and shape each portion into a ball. On a clean work surface, use a rolling pin to roll the balls into very thin cutlets, about ¼ inch (6mm) thick. Place the cutlets in the boiling liquid and boil over medium-high heat for 30 minutes, until most of the liquid is absorbed and the cutlets are puffy and have increased in size.

4. When the seitan is done, remove it from the pot and allow to cool for 5 to 10 minutes. If some of the cutlets have broken into smaller pieces, that's fine.

5. In a sauté pan, melt the vegan butter and oil over medium heat for 1 minute. Add the onion and garlic and sauté for 5 minutes.

6. Meanwhile, pour the flour onto a plate. Dredge both sides of the seitan cutlets and any broken pieces in the flour. Place in the pan with the onion and garlic and pan-fry, still over medium heat, for 5 minutes per side, until golden brown. If the pan seems too dry, add another ½ tablespoon of vegan butter. When the cutlets are done, remove them from the pan.

7. Reduce the heat under the sauté pan to low. Pour in the Marsala wine and broth and stir. Then add the sugar, salt, and pepper and stir to combine.

8. In a small bowl, mix the cornstarch with 1 tablespoon of water to create a slurry. Pour the slurry into the pan.

If you'd like, add 6 ounces (170g) of halved cremini mushrooms along with the onion and garlic in Step 5. Sauté until soft, 5 to 7 minutes.

9. Simmer the sauce over medium heat for 5 to 7 minutes, until thickened. Once thickened, return the seitan cutlets to the pan and simmer for 2 minutes to allow the seitan to soak up some of the sauce.

10. Garnish with a few parsley leaves and a pinch of salt and pepper and serve.

spinach and tofu ricotta–stuffed shells

Yield: 4 servings

Prep Time: 20 minutes
(not including time to make
tomato sauce and tofu ricotta)

Cook Time: 40 minutes

Jumbo pasta shells stuffed with a creamy, cheesy filling and baked until crispy on the outside and melty on the inside are a perfect weeknight meal. This family-friendly dish comes together very quickly, and you will probably have leftovers for lunch the next day! I would pair it with a simple side salad and some bread for a delicious and satisfying meal.

20 jumbo pasta shells (about 6 ounces/170g)

6 ounces (170g) fresh spinach, roughly chopped

2 cloves garlic, minced

1½ teaspoons olive oil

1 batch Tomato Sauce (page 189)

1 batch Tofu Ricotta (page 188)

¾ cup (84g) vegan mozzarella shreds, divided

Salt

A few fresh parsley leaves, for garnish

To reheat leftovers, you can microwave them or place them in a preheated 350°F (176°C) oven for 15 to 20 minutes, until warmed through. Serve with extra sauce.

1. Preheat the oven to 400°F (204°C).

2. Bring a large pot of salted water to a boil over high heat. Add the pasta shells and cook until just slightly undercooked, or 1 to 2 minutes less than the suggested cooking time on the package. The pasta will still be a little hard at the very center. (You want to undercook them slightly because they will continue to cook in the oven.)

3. Meanwhile, in a medium-sized nonstick frying pan over medium heat, sauté the spinach and garlic in the oil for 5 minutes, or until the spinach is wilted.

4. Pour 1 cup (255g) of the tomato sauce into a 9 by 11-inch (23 by 28cm) baking dish. Spread with a spoon to evenly coat the bottom.

5. In a medium-sized bowl, mix together the sautéed spinach and garlic, the tofu ricotta, and ½ cup (56g) of the vegan mozzarella shreds. Season with salt to taste.

6. When the shells are done, drain them. Carefully scoop 1½ tablespoons of the filling into each shell. Place the stuffed shells in the baking dish.

7. Drizzle ½ cup (112g) of the tomato sauce over the shells and sprinkle the remaining mozzarella shreds over the top. Bake the shells for 25 minutes, or until crispy around the edges and the vegan cheese is melted.

8. Allow to rest for 5 minutes before serving. While the shells are resting, warm the remaining tomato sauce in a small saucepan.

9. Garnish the stuffed shells with a few parsley leaves and serve with the warm sauce.

white chick'n chili

Yield: 4 servings

Prep Time: 20 minutes,
plus time to soak cashews

Cook Time: 35 minutes

A variation on regular tomato-based chili, this vegan chili is creamy, cheesy, and less spicy. It is perfect for a cold night. If you prefer your chili spicier, double the amount of pickled jalapeños to give this dish a real kick. Don't forget to soak the cashews the night before so that they will be ready to use when you're ready to make the chili! A high-powered blender is important for making the cashew cream smooth.

¼ onion (about 2 ounces/55g), chopped

1 clove garlic, minced

1½ teaspoons olive oil

1 cup (100g) textured vegetable protein (TVP)

¾ cup (90g) raw cashews, soaked in water overnight, drained, and rinsed

1 cup (240ml) nondairy milk

2 cups (475ml) low-sodium vegetable broth

1 (15½-ounce/439g) can cannellini beans, drained and rinsed

1 (15½-ounce/439g) can pinto beans, drained and rinsed

⅓ cup (37g) vegan mozzarella shreds, plus more for topping

¼ cup (40g) pickled jalapeños, chopped

½ teaspoon chili powder

¼ teaspoon salt

Leaves from 2 to 3 sprigs fresh cilantro, for garnish

4 lime slices, for garnish

¼ cup (60g) vegan sour cream, divided, for garnish

SPECIAL EQUIPMENT:
High-powered blender

1. Place the TVP in a bowl and pour 1 cup (240ml) of water over it. Set aside for 10 minutes to rehydrate.

2. In a large pot, cook the onion and garlic in the oil over low heat for 5 minutes, or until fragrant.

3. Meanwhile, put the soaked cashews and nondairy milk in a high-powered blender and blend until very smooth. The mixture will be thick and resemble heavy cream. Pour it into the pot with the onion and garlic.

4. Increase the heat under the pot to medium-high. Add the broth, beans, vegan mozzarella shreds, jalapeños, chili powder, salt, and rehydrated TVP and mix with a large spoon. When the vegan cheese has fully melted, reduce the heat and simmer the chili for 15 to 20 minutes, until thickened. As it cools, it will thicken further.

5. To serve, divide the chili among 4 bowls and garnish each bowl with cilantro leaves, a lime slice, 1 tablespoon of vegan sour cream, and a sprinkle of vegan mozzarella shreds.

vegan mac and cheese

Yield: 6 to 8 servings

Prep Time: 5 minutes

Cook Time: 20 minutes

Nothing beats a good macaroni and cheese, a classic and comforting dish. There are a lot of ways to make vegan mac and cheese, but I promise this is the best way. Given how creamy this version is, you will be amazed that there is no dairy in it! Elbow macaroni is definitely the preferred pasta for mac and cheese, but you can use any pasta you like.

1 (16-ounce/454g) box elbow macaroni

¼ cup (56g) vegan butter

¼ cup (30g) all-purpose flour

3 cups (710ml) nondairy milk

½ cup (4 ounces/115g) vegan cream cheese

1 cup (112g) vegan cheddar shreds

1 cup (112g) vegan mozzarella shreds

1 tablespoon nutritional yeast

½ teaspoon salt

½ teaspoon garlic powder

¼ teaspoon paprika

Dash of ground black pepper

1.   Bring a large pot of salted water to a boil. Add the macaroni and cook for 10 to 12 minutes, or 1 to 2 minutes past the cooking time indicated on the package for al dente. The pasta should be soft but not mushy. Reserve ¼ cup (60ml) of the starchy cooking water, then drain the pasta and return it to the pot.

2.   Meanwhile, melt the vegan butter in a medium-sized saucepan over medium-low heat. Add the flour and whisk to form a roux.

3.   When the vegan butter has absorbed the flour, slowly pour in the nondairy milk, about 1 cup (240ml) at a time, whisking to prevent clumping.

4.   Add the vegan cream cheese, vegan cheese shreds, nutritional yeast, salt, and spices and stir to combine. Reduce the heat to low and continue to cook until all of the cheese has melted.

5.   Place the pot with the drained pasta over low heat and pour the cheese sauce and reserved pasta cooking water over the pasta. Stir until the macaroni is evenly coated. Serve immediately.

cobb salad with vegan buttermilk ranch dressing

Yield: 4 servings

Prep Time: 10 minutes
(not including time to make
tempeh bacon or dressing)

This nontraditional take on Cobb salad combines classic elements like vegan bacon and avocado with fun additions like corn and chickpeas. A creamy dressing pulls it all together. I imagine eating this salad on a warm spring day with a glass of lemon iced tea—sounds perfect!

3 romaine hearts, finely chopped

1 Hass avocado, sliced

1 (15½-ounce/439g) can chickpeas, drained and rinsed

1½ cups (200g) frozen corn, thawed

¼ cup (45g) finely chopped red onions

1½ batches Tempeh Bacon Crumbles (page 186)

1 batch Vegan Buttermilk Ranch Dressing (page 187)

Place the chopped romaine in a large bowl. Top the lettuce in sections with the avocado slices, chickpeas, corn, red onions, and tempeh bacon crumbles. Drizzle the dressing over the salad. If you prefer, you can save some dressing to serve on the side.

creamy "beefy" shells

Yield: 4 servings
Prep Time: 10 minutes
Cook Time: 25 minutes

This meal is so easy to make and comes together so quickly that it is likely to become a new favorite in your house. The creamy, "beefy" sauce makes this such a comforting dish. Serve it with a salad and some bread for an instant dinner!

8 ounces (225g) medium pasta shells

¼ onion, preferably Vidalia (about 2 ounces/55g), chopped

2 cloves garlic, minced

1 tablespoon olive oil

1 tablespoon vegan butter

1 pound (454g) vegan ground beef

1 (6-ounce/170g) can tomato paste

1 cup (240ml) nondairy milk

1 cup (112g) vegan mozzarella shreds

½ teaspoon organic granulated sugar

Salt

4 leaves fresh parsley, chopped, for garnish

1. Bring a large pot of salted water to a boil. Add the pasta shells and cook according to the package instructions for al dente. Reserve 1 cup (240ml) of the starchy cooking water, then drain the pasta.

2. Meanwhile, sauté the onion and garlic in the oil and vegan butter in a large nonstick frying pan or cast-iron skillet over medium heat for 3 minutes, or until fragrant.

3. Add the vegan ground beef to the pan with the onion and garlic and continue to cook over medium heat, stirring occasionally with a rubber spatula or wooden spoon, for 8 minutes, or until the vegan ground beef starts to brown.

4. Scoop the tomato paste into the pan and stir to coat everything in the tomato paste.

5. Add the nondairy milk, vegan mozzarella shreds, and sugar and stir until the shreds have melted and the ingredients are well incorporated. The sauce will be smooth and creamy.

6. Pour the cooked pasta into the pan along with three-quarters of the reserved pasta water. Stir to coat the shells evenly. Cook over medium heat for 1 minute, or until the pasta has absorbed the liquid and the sauce is thick and shiny. If the sauce looks dry, slowly add the remaining ¼ cup (60ml) of pasta water and stir. Before serving, taste and add salt as needed.

7. Garnish with a sprinkle of fresh parsley and serve.

homemade gnocchi with vegan butter thyme sauce

Yield: 4 servings

Prep Time: 30 minutes

Cook Time: 1 hour 10 minutes

Gnocchi are one of my favorite pastas. They are more akin to dumplings than pasta (gnocchi is Italian for "dumplings"). They are almost always used fresh, and they have a delicate, silky smooth texture while being satisfyingly dense, the way all good dumplings are. Homemade gnocchi are easy to prepare and require only a few simple ingredients: flour, potatoes, and salt. There are many ways of making gnocchi. You can use different flours, sweet potatoes, cauliflower, vegan ricotta—the list goes on. This classic recipe results in light, fluffy little dumplings. Paired with a light vegan butter thyme sauce, they are irresistible.

GNOCCHI

4 small russet potatoes (about 1½ pounds/680g)

1¼ cups (150g) all-purpose flour, plus more for dusting

¼ teaspoon salt

VEGAN BUTTER THYME SAUCE

2 tablespoons vegan butter

1 tablespoon olive oil

2 cloves garlic, minced

Leaves from 3 to 4 sprigs fresh thyme

1. Preheat the oven to 450°F (232°C).

2. Wash the potatoes and pierce them all over with a fork. Wrap them in aluminum foil and bake for 1 hour, or until soft. Remove from the oven and their foil packets, then allow to cool for 5 minutes before handling.

3. Cut each potato in half crosswise, then carefully peel off the skins. You can do this with your fingers or a spoon, but be careful because the potatoes will still be hot. Place the peeled potatoes in a large bowl.

4. Use a potato ricer or masher or the back of a fork to mash the potatoes until very smooth. This is important because the potatoes need to be broken down as much as possible.

5. Slowly pour in ½ cup (60g) of the flour and the salt and mix with a fork until shaggy pieces form; then begin to knead the dough with your hands. Add the remaining flour in ½-cup (60g) increments, kneading after each addition to work in the flour, until you have a dough that is soft but no longer sticky or tacky. (See note, opposite.)

6. Turn the dough out onto a clean, lightly floured surface and shape it into a small loaf around 5 inches (12.7cm) long. Cut the loaf into 5 equal pieces.

7. Use your hands to roll a piece of the dough into a log that's 14 to 19 inches (35 to 48cm) in length and about 1 inch (2.5cm) in diameter. Cut the log crosswise into 1-inch (2.5cm) pieces for the gnocchi. Sprinkle a rimmed baking sheet with flour.

8. Take a 1-inch (2.5cm) piece of dough and roll it into a cylinder. If you like, use the back of a fork to press down gently and create the ribbed effect shown in the photos. Repeat with

The key to light and fluffy gnocchi is not to add too much flour. The more times you make gnocchi, the more you will learn how much flour you need. If this is your first time making gnocchi, I suggest you get a kitchen scale and follow this recipe according to weight. The weight of the peeled potatoes after baking was 15½ ounces (435g). If your potatoes weigh more or less, you can adjust the quantity of flour, which is why it is important to incorporate the flour gradually. The dough should be soft and light, and it shouldn't be at all sticky. If you find it is sticking because it's still wet, continue to add more flour in ¼-cup (30g) increments.

the remaining 1-inch (2.5cm) dough pieces. Place the formed gnocchi on the prepared baking sheet and cover with a clean kitchen towel. Repeat with the remaining 4 pieces of dough to form the rest of the gnocchi.

9.   Bring a large pot of salted water to a boil. Drop the gnocchi into the boiling water and cook for 3 to 5 minutes, or until they float to the top.

10. Meanwhile, make the sauce: In a large frying pan, melt the vegan butter with the oil over low heat. Add the garlic and thyme and cook, stirring occasionally, while the gnocchi cook.

11. When the gnocchi are done, use a slotted spoon to transfer them to the pan with the sauce. You want little bits of pasta water to get tossed in with the gnocchi to help thicken the sauce. After you've transferred all of the gnocchi to the pan, carefully toss to coat in the sauce and add salt to taste. Serve immediately.

kale, white bean, and vegan sausage skillet

Yield: 4 servings
Prep Time: 10 minutes
Cook Time: 30 minutes

A variation on regular chili, this vegan chili is creamy, cheesy, and less spicy. It is perfect for cold nights. If you prefer your food spicier, double the amount of pickled jalapeño to add a real kick to this dish. Soak the cashews the night before, and then they will be ready to use when you are ready to make the chili. A high-powered blender is important for making the cashew cream smooth.

1 bunch kale (about 8½ ounces/240g), destemmed and chopped

2 (15½-ounce/439g) cans cannellini beans, undrained

2 cloves garlic, minced

Juice of ½ lemon

1 tablespoon olive oil

4 Italian-style vegan sausages, sliced

¼ teaspoon red pepper flakes, or to taste

Salt

1 tablespoon shredded or grated vegan parmesan, for topping

SPECIAL EQUIPMENT:
High-powered blender

1. Put the kale in a large nonstick frying pan and pour in 1 cup (240ml) of water. Cover with a lid and steam over medium-high heat for 10 minutes, or until the kale is mostly tender and has turned a bit darker in color.

2. Pour in the beans and liquid from the cans and add the garlic. Mix everything together with a spoon. Stir in the lemon juice.

3. Reduce the heat to medium and cook the kale and beans for 10 minutes, stirring occasionally, until the kale is extremely tender and dark green and the beans are soft.

4. Meanwhile, in a medium-sized nonstick frying pan, heat the oil over medium heat. Add the vegan sausage slices and pan-fry until crispy, about 10 minutes.

5. Transfer the sausages to the pan with the kale mixture and stir. Add the red pepper flakes and salt according to taste. Sprinkle with the vegan parmesan and serve immediately.

140   4. Mains

vegan philly "cheese steak"

Yield: 4 sandwiches
Prep Time: 20 minutes
Cook Time: 50 minutes

A traditional Philly cheese steak is made from thinly sliced pieces of steak topped with cheese sauce. Sometimes it is paired with grilled peppers and onions. This vegan version replaces the steak with seitan, and it's incredibly delicious. Pair it with a side of fries and a cold soda for maximum fast-food feels!

SEITAN

2 tablespoons low-sodium soy sauce

1 tablespoon plus ¼ teaspoon seasoning salt, divided

2 bay leaves

1 cup (120g) vital wheat gluten

1 tablespoon garlic powder

1 tablespoon onion powder

1 green or red bell pepper (about 6 ounces/170g), thinly sliced

1 medium onion, preferably Vidalia (about 6 ounces/170g), thinly sliced

1 tablespoon plus 1½ teaspoons olive oil, divided

2 teaspoons low-sodium soy sauce

1½ teaspoons garlic powder

1½ teaspoons onion powder

Salt and pepper, to taste

CHEESY SAUCE

3 ounces (85g) vegan cheddar shreds

½ cup (120ml) nondairy milk, plus more as needed

4 hoagie-style rolls

1. Prepare the cooking broth for the seitan: Fill a large pot with 2 quarts (2L) of water and add 1 tablespoon of the seasoning salt and the bay leaves. Bring to a boil over high heat.

2. Meanwhile, prepare the seitan mixture: In a large bowl, mix the vital wheat gluten with the garlic powder, onion powder, and remaining ¼ teaspoon of seasoning salt. Pour in ½ cup (120ml) of water and stir to combine. Use your hands to knead the mixture for 3 minutes, or until a soft, spongy dough has formed. If you can see dry spots, gradually add more water in 1-tablespoon increments. Form the dough into a small loaf, about 5 inches (12.7cm) long and 2 inches (5cm) thick.

3. Carefully place the seitan log in the pot of boiling broth and boil for 30 minutes, until the seitan is puffy. You can save any leftover broth for soups or discard it.

4. When the seitan has 15 minutes left to boil, sauté the pepper and onion in 1 tablespoon of the oil in a large nonstick frying pan over medium heat for 15 to 20 minutes, or until softened.

5. Use a slotted spoon or tongs to transfer the seitan from the pot to a cutting board and allow to cool for 5 minutes. With a sharp knife, cut the seitan into very thin slices—as thin as you can cut it. If the slices are very long, cut them in half to make smaller pieces.

6. Transfer the pepper and onion to a bowl. Pour the remaining 1½ teaspoons of oil into the same frying pan, then add the sliced seitan and pan-fry over medium heat for 10 minutes, until crispy and browned.

7. Meanwhile, prepare the cheesy sauce: Put the ingredients in a small saucepan and cook over low heat, stirring frequently, until the sauce is smooth, about 8 minutes. If necessary, add more nondairy milk to thin it out.

In this recipe, seasoning salt is used to add extra flavor and dimension to the seitan. Seasoning salt is a blend of salt and seasonings, such as garlic powder, onion powder, black pepper, and more. I prefer the one from Trader Joe's, but any seasoning salt is great.

If you prefer the rolls to be toasted, place them in a preheated 350°F (176°C) oven for 5 to 10 minutes, until crisp and golden, and then assemble the sandwiches.

8. Pour the soy sauce into the pan with the seitan and toss to coat the pieces evenly. Sprinkle with the garlic powder and onion powder and toss to coat. Return the pepper and onion to the pan and toss everything together. Before serving, taste and add salt and pepper as needed.

9. To assemble the sandwiches, evenly divide the seitan, pepper, and onion mixture among the rolls, then drizzle with the cheesy sauce. Enjoy immediately.

creamy lemon pasta

Yield: 4 to 6 servings

Prep Time: 10 minutes, plus time to soak cashews

Cook Time: 20 minutes

This pasta dish includes only a few simple ingredients, but it tastes incredible. The creamy sauce is filled with garlic and lemon flavors, which pair perfectly with a long, flat noodle like tagliatelle. If you can't find tagliatelle, fettuccine or rigatoni would also be great; really, you can use any pasta you like. An important trick when making pasta is to save some of the cooking water. It helps the sauce adhere to the pasta and, because of the starch content, thins the sauce without making it as runny as regular water would.

12 ounces (340g) tagliatelle pasta

¾ cup (90g) raw cashews, soaked overnight, rinsed, and drained

¾ cup (180ml) nondairy milk

1 tablespoon olive oil

1 tablespoon vegan butter

2 cloves garlic, minced

Grated zest of 1 lemon, plus more for garnish

Juice of 3 lemons

¼ cup (28g) shredded or grated vegan parmesan, plus more for garnish

Salt

4 to 6 lemon slices, for garnish

SPECIAL EQUIPMENT:
High-powered blender

1. Bring a large pot of salted water to a boil. Add the pasta and cook according to the package instructions for al dente.

2. Meanwhile, put the cashews and nondairy milk in a high-powered blender. Blend on high speed for 1 minute, until the cashews are fully broken down and the mixture is creamy and smooth.

3. Place the oil, vegan butter, and garlic in a large sauté pan over medium heat. Sauté the garlic for 3 minutes, or until fragrant.

4. Pour the cashew cream into the sauté pan, then add the lemon zest and juice and vegan parmesan. Reduce the heat to low, mix with a wooden spoon, and cook until the pasta is done.

5. Scoop out 1 cup (240ml) of the pasta cooking water, then pour ½ cup (120ml) of it into the sauce and stir. Drain the pasta and pour it into the pan with the sauce.

6. Using tongs or a spoon, toss the pasta to coat it in the sauce. If it seems too dry, add more of the reserved pasta water. The sauce should be creamy, smooth, and thick and should coat the pasta evenly. Before serving, taste the pasta and add salt as needed.

7. Place a large twirl of pasta on a plate. Sprinkle with extra lemon zest and vegan parmesan and serve with a lemon slice.

taco casserole

Yield: 4 servings
Prep Time: 10 minutes
Cook Time: 1 hour

This casserole is a fun play on the flavors and textures of tacos. It comes together easily and makes a perfect weeknight dinner because the oven does most of the work! Feel free to customize it by adding any taco toppings you like. Serve it with a side of Perfect White Rice (page 191) and you have a delicious meal!

⅓ cup (65g) chopped onions, preferably Vidalia

1 tablespoon olive oil

1 (15½-ounce/439g) can black beans, drained and rinsed

1 pound (454g) vegan ground beef

1½ tablespoons taco seasoning, divided

1 (6-ounce/170g) can tomato paste

½ teaspoon organic granulated sugar

¼ teaspoon red pepper flakes, or to taste

Salt

⅔ cup (90g) frozen corn

¾ cup (84g) vegan cheddar shreds

½ cup (120g) vegan sour cream

2 ounces (55g) tortilla chips, crushed

1 cup (60g) shredded lettuce

1 (2¼-ounce/64g) can sliced black olives

1. Preheat the oven to 375°F (190°C).

2. In a large nonstick frying pan, sauté the onions in the oil over medium heat for 3 minutes, or until translucent. Add the beans, vegan ground beef, and 1 tablespoon of the taco seasoning. Sauté for 8 more minutes, until the vegan beef starts to brown.

3. Turn off the heat, pour in ½ cup (120ml) of water, and stir. The vegan ground beef and beans will absorb the water to make a thick, saucy mixture.

4. Meanwhile, in a separate bowl, mix together the tomato paste, sugar, 1 cup (240ml) of water, and the remaining ½ tablespoon of taco seasoning. Stir until the sauce is smooth. Taste the sauce and add the red pepper flakes and salt according to taste.

5. Pour three-quarters of the tomato sauce into an 8-inch (20cm) square baking dish. Spread with a spoon to evenly coat the bottom. Spoon half of the bean and vegan ground beef mixture over the sauce. Sprinkle the corn over the top, then add the remaining bean and vegan beef mixture. Top with the vegan cheddar shreds.

6. Cover with aluminum foil and bake for 40 minutes, or until the casserole is bubbly and the vegan cheese has melted.

7. Meanwhile, place the vegan sour cream and 1 tablespoon of water in a medium-sized bowl and mix to combine. Set aside.

8. Remove the casserole from the oven and remove the foil. Sprinkle the casserole with the crushed tortilla chips. Return the dish to the oven and bake for 8 more minutes, uncovered. The chips will start to absorb some of the sauce and melted vegan cheese. Do not let the chips burn.

9. Sprinkle the lettuce and sliced olives over the casserole and drizzle with the vegan sour cream. Serve with the remaining tomato sauce.

chick'n and dumplings

Yield: 4 servings
Prep Time: 15 minutes
Cook Time: 40 minutes

This traditional Southern dish is typically prepared with chicken in a creamy broth. In this recipe, soy curls are used as a replacement. They come dehydrated, and you can find them online. The dumplings are actually biscuit dough that is steamed right in the soup. All of the elements working together make this dish the true essence of comfort food.

SOUP

2 tablespoons olive oil

2 carrots (about 4 ounces/115g), sliced

2 celery ribs, chopped (about 5 ounces/140g)

2 cloves garlic, chopped

¼ onion (about 2 ounces/55g), chopped

10 cups (2.4L) low-sodium vegetable broth

2 bay leaves

2 tablespoons vegan butter

¼ teaspoon salt

¼ teaspoon ground black pepper

½ cup (60g) all-purpose flour

1½ cups (60g) dehydrated soy curls

¼ cup (15g) chopped fresh parsley

DUMPLINGS

2 cups (240g) all-purpose flour

2 teaspoons baking powder

1 teaspoon salt

⅔ cup (160ml) nondairy milk

2 tablespoons vegan butter, melted

1. Make the soup: Heat the oil in a 6-quart (5.7L) pot over medium heat. Add the carrots, celery, garlic, and onion and sauté for 5 minutes, or until the vegetables are fragrant. Pour in the broth and stir to combine. Tie the bay leaves together and place them in the pot along with the vegan butter, salt, and pepper. Bring to a boil over high heat, then continue to boil for 8 to 10 minutes, until the soup is very hot and the vegetables have softened.

2. Carefully scoop out 2 cups of the soup broth and whisk it with the flour in a large bowl to make a slurry. Remove and discard the bay leaves. Pour the slurry into the soup (this will help thicken it) and reduce the heat to medium. Add the soy curls and parsley and stir. Simmer over medium heat for 5 to 7 minutes, until the soy curls are rehydrated and soft.

3. Meanwhile, prepare the dumplings: In a large bowl, whisk together the flour, baking powder, and salt. Pour in the nondairy milk and melted vegan butter and mix with a spoon to form a sticky dough.

4. Scoop 2 heaping tablespoons of the dough into the simmering soup to form a dumpling. Repeat until all of the dough has been used; you should get 12 dumplings total.

5. Cover the pot with a lid and simmer the soup over medium heat for 15 minutes. The dumplings will puff up during cooking; if you cut one in half, it should look like a dry biscuit.

6. To serve, place 3 dumplings in each bowl and pour one-quarter of the soup over the dumplings. Garnish each serving with a pinch of black pepper.

minestrone

Yield: 4 servings
Prep Time: 15 minutes
Cook Time: 35 minutes

Minestrone is such a classic soup because it is hearty, comforting, and easy to make. While this soup is simple, it has a lot of flavor and is a great way to get your vegetables in. This is one of my favorite dinners during the winter.

2 carrots (about 4¼ ounces/ 120g), chopped

2 celery ribs (about 5 ounces/ 140g), chopped

3 cloves garlic, minced

½ onion (about 4 ounces/112g), chopped

2 tablespoons olive oil

7 cups (1660ml) low-sodium vegetable broth

2 cups (488g) crushed tomatoes

2 (15½-ounce/439g) cans kidney beans, drained and rinsed

4 small Yukon Gold potatoes (about 11 ounces/310g), chopped

12 ounces (340g) penne pasta

4 cups (113g) spinach

Salt and pepper

Leaves from 2 sprigs fresh parsley, for garnish

1. In a large pot, sauté the carrots, celery, and garlic in the oil over medium-low heat for 5 minutes, until the onions turn translucent and the garlic becomes fragrant.

2. Pour the broth and tomatoes into the pot. Mix with a spoon.

3. Add the beans and potatoes and increase the heat to medium-high. Bring the soup to a simmer. Once simmering, reduce the heat to medium to maintain a simmer (do not boil). Simmer uncovered for 20 minutes, or until the potatoes are soft.

4. In a separate pot, boil the pasta according to the package instructions for al dente. Drain.

5. Once the potatoes are soft, add the pasta and spinach to the soup. Simmer for 3 more minutes, until the spinach is wilted. Season with salt and pepper to taste.

6. To serve, ladle into soup bowls and garnish with a few parsley leaves and a little salt and pepper.

5.

desserts

Looking for something to satisfy your sweet tooth? You've come to the right place. This chapter covers everything from cakes to cookies to pies and more. There really is something for everyone. Whether you love to bake or you just want cookies on a lazy Sunday, all of these recipes are amazing.

While some of these desserts may be a bit time-intensive—I'm looking at you, Mini Salted Caramel "Cheesecake" and Rainbow Cookies—nothing is too difficult. There are also good classic recipes in this chapter, like the Strawberry Shortcake and Iced Sugar Cookies. All of them are perfect to have in your arsenal of easy but incredibly delicious vegan desserts.

arroz con leche

Yield: 6 to 8 servings
Prep Time: 5 minutes
Cook Time: 40 minutes

The Spanish rendition of rice pudding is made with milk and cinnamon to create an incredibly delicious dessert. Even though this version is vegan, it is just as creamy as the original and has just the right amount of sweetness. It is easy to make and can be enjoyed hot or cold, although you may find it hard to resist eating it straight out of the pan. I prefer to use almond milk in this recipe, but you can use whichever nondairy milk you prefer.

1½ cups (270g) long-grain white rice

1½ teaspoons ground cinnamon, divided

1 (13½-ounce/400ml) can full-fat coconut milk

1 cup (240ml) sweetened nondairy milk

¼ cup (48g) organic granulated sugar

2 tablespoons maple syrup

1 tablespoon vanilla extract

TOPPINGS (per serving)

½ banana, sliced

5 strawberries, quartered

2 tablespoons sweetened shredded coconut

¼ teaspoon ground cinnamon

1 tablespoon maple syrup

1 tablespoon sweetened nondairy milk

1. Pour 4½ cups (1.1L) of water into a large saucepan. Add the rice and 1 teaspoon of the cinnamon and bring to a boil over high heat. Continue to boil, uncovered, for 18 minutes, or until the water is completely absorbed.

2. Turn off the heat and pour in the coconut milk, nondairy milk, sugar, maple syrup, vanilla extract, and remaining ½ teaspoon of cinnamon. Use a spoon to mix until well combined. The rice will begin to absorb a bit of the liquid.

3. Simmer uncovered over low heat for 18 to 20 minutes, stirring frequently and making sure the rice is not sticking to the bottom of the pan, until the pudding is very thick and creamy.

4. Enjoy hot or cold. When ready to serve, top with the banana slices, quartered strawberries, shredded coconut, cinnamon, maple syrup, and nondairy milk.

Sweetened condensed milk is sometimes included in recipes for rice pudding. Here, I use sweetened nondairy milk to approximate that sweetness.

baked apple empanadas

Yield: 15 empanadas
(5 to 7 servings)

Prep Time: 35 minutes, plus
30 minutes to chill dough

Cook Time: 30 minutes

If you love apple pie, then you are going to adore these apple empanadas, which are basically a miniature version of apple pies. Empanadas are usually fried, but baking them is easier, and they still come out crispy and golden. These are delicious on their own, or you can serve them with some vegan ice cream or vegan whipped cream.

DOUGH

1½ cups (180g) all-purpose flour, plus more for dusting

1 tablespoon organic granulated sugar

¼ teaspoon salt

½ cup (112g) cold vegan butter

FILLING

2 large Granny Smith apples (about 15 ounces/425g), peeled and diced

1 tablespoon lemon juice

2 tablespoons all-purpose flour

¼ cup (48g) organic dark brown sugar

2 tablespoons organic granulated sugar

1½ teaspoons ground cinnamon

1½ teaspoons vanilla extract

FOR TOPPING

1 tablespoon organic confectioners' sugar

1 tablespoon organic dark brown sugar

1. Prepare the dough: In a large bowl, whisk together the flour, sugar, and salt. Cut the vegan butter into the flour mixture using a fork or pastry cutter until small, crumbly pieces have formed. Slowly pour in 3 tablespoons of water and continue to mix. The dough will start to become shaggy. Knead with your hands for 3 to 5 minutes, until the dough forms a smooth ball. Place in the refrigerator to chill for 30 minutes.

2. Prepare the filling: Put the apples in a large bowl. Pour the lemon juice over the apples and toss to coat. Sprinkle with the flour, sugars, cinnamon, and vanilla extract. Toss to coat.

3. Preheat the oven to 375°F (190°C). Line a rimmed baking sheet with parchment paper.

4. Remove the dough from the refrigerator, place it on a lightly floured surface, and roll it out into a large circle about ¼ inch (6mm) thick. Using a biscuit cutter or a large cup, cut out 3-inch (8cm) circles. Work the scraps into a ball, roll it out again, and cut additional circles until all of the dough has been used. You should get a total of 15 dough circles.

5. Lightly pat down a dough circle with your hands to stretch it out a bit. Scoop 1½ to 2 tablespoons of the filling onto half of the circle and form the filling into a little log shape. Fold the other half of the dough over the filling. To seal the empanada, crimp the edges with a fork. Place on the lined baking sheet and repeat until all of the empanadas have been made.

6. At the bottom of the bowl in which you made the filling, there will be some liquid. Use a silicone basting brush to brush this liquid over the empanadas.

7. Bake the empanadas for 25 to 30 minutes, until golden brown and crispy. Top with the sugars and serve.

vanilla cupcakes with vanilla buttercream

Yield: 12 cupcakes

Prep Time: 25 minutes, plus time to cool

Cook Time: 20 minutes

Don't let this all-vanilla cupcake fool you into thinking it's boring. It is light, fluffy, sweet (but not too sweet), and everything you want a cupcake to be. I guarantee, people will be asking you to make these on repeat. My dad, who isn't vegan and typically doesn't like desserts, ate three of these cupcakes and then talked about them for days! While I love the simplicity of these cupcakes, they're also a great base for adding sprinkles and other toppings.

2 egg replacers (see pages 11–12)

¾ cup (180ml) nondairy milk

½ cup (120g) vegan sour cream

½ cup (112g) vegan butter, melted

1 teaspoon vanilla extract

1½ cups (180g) all-purpose flour, sifted

¾ cup (145g) organic granulated sugar

1½ teaspoons baking powder

VANILLA BUTTERCREAM

1 cup (224g) vegan butter, softened

1 teaspoon vanilla extract

3 cups (360g) organic confectioners' sugar, sifted

2 tablespoons nondairy milk

1. Preheat the oven to 350°F (176°C). Place 12 paper liners in a standard-size muffin pan.

2. Put the egg replacers, nondairy milk, vegan sour cream, melted vegan butter, and vanilla extract in a large bowl. Use an electric mixer to beat on medium speed for 30 seconds, until light and fluffy.

3. Add the flour, granulated sugar, and baking powder to the bowl with the wet ingredients and mix on low speed for 15 to 20 seconds, then increase the speed to medium and mix for 40 to 60 more seconds, just until well combined. Do not overmix. If necessary, scrape down the sides of the bowl with a rubber spatula.

4. Divide the batter evenly among the lined wells of the muffin pan, filling each well three-quarters full.

5. Bake for 15 to 20 minutes, until the edges of the cupcakes are slightly golden and a toothpick inserted in the center of a cupcake comes out clean.

6. Transfer the cupcakes to a wire rack and let cool for at least 1 hour or overnight (see note, opposite) before frosting.

7. Meanwhile, prepare the vanilla buttercream: Place the vegan butter in a large bowl and use an electric mixer to beat on medium speed for 2 to 3 minutes, until very soft and fluffy. Add the vanilla extract and gradually add the confectioners' sugar while mixing on medium speed. After all of the sugar is incorporated, pour in the nondairy milk and beat on high for 3 to 5 minutes, scraping down the sides of the bowl occasionally to make sure everything is well combined. The frosting will be pale, light, and fluffy.

You can make these cupcakes a day ahead and frost them the next day if you like. Store the cooled, unfrosted cupcakes in an airtight container on the counter overnight.

8.   When the cupcakes are completely cool, place the frosting in a piping bag or a plastic bag with a corner snipped off and frost the cupcakes. (I used a Wilton 1M tip to create the swirls.) Alternatively, you can use a small knife or an offset spatula to spread the frosting on the cupcakes. Store leftover frosted cupcakes on a plate, covered with aluminum foil, on the counter for up to 2 days.

banana pudding pie

Yield: 6 to 8 servings

Prep Time: 20 minutes, plus at least 4 hours to chill

An easy homemade cookie crust filled with delicious banana pudding and topped with light, fluffy Cocowhip makes this no-bake dessert a dream. This pie has always been a hit with my family; we serve it at most parties. Believe it or not, boxed pudding mix is typically vegan, but be sure to double-check the ingredients. This pie must be refrigerated until it is served. Don't worry if it gets a little messy; it will still be delicious.

CRUST

28 vegan golden sandwich cookies

¼ cup (56g) vegan butter, melted

PUDDING

2 (3.4-ounce/96g) boxes instant banana cream pudding

2 cups plus 1 tablespoon (495ml) nondairy milk

TOPPING

¾ cup (175g) Cocowhip coconut whipped topping

2 vegan golden sandwich cookies

1 banana (about 3 ounces/85g), sliced on a bias

SPECIAL EQUIPMENT:
High-powered blender

1. Prepare the crust: In a high-powered blender or food processor, blend the 28 cookies until they form a fine crumb. You may need to scrape down the sides with a rubber spatula. Pour the crumbs into a 9-inch (23cm) pie dish. Pour the melted vegan butter on top and mix with a spoon until well combined. Use your hands to press the crumbs into the bottom and up the sides of the dish, then use a flat-bottomed glass or measuring cup to press it down.

2. Prepare the pudding: Put the ingredients in a large container and shake for 2 to 3 minutes, until pudding forms. If there are clumps when you open the container, mix the pudding with a spoon to break them up.

3. Pour the pudding into the pie crust. Cover the pie and refrigerate for at least 4 hours or overnight.

4. Spread the coconut whipped topping over the top of the pie. Blend the 2 cookies into fine crumbs as you did in Step 1. Arrange the banana slices on top of the pie, then sprinkle with the cookie crumbs. Cut into slices and serve.

fudgy brownies

Yield: 16 (2-inch/5cm) brownies

Prep Time: 15 minutes, plus time to cool

Cook Time: 20 minutes

Move over, boxed brownie mixes, because we are going to make them from scratch. These soft, chewy, and delicious brownies contain a secret ingredient—tahini! Tahini is made from ground sesame seeds, and it's a great source of healthy fats. Get ready for your house to smell like chocolate heaven!

¾ cup (145g) organic granulated sugar

¼ cup (48g) organic dark brown sugar

¼ cup (64g) tahini

¼ cup (56g) vegan butter, melted and hot

¼ heaping cup (70g) vegan semisweet chocolate chips, melted

2 egg replacers (see pages 11–12)

1 teaspoon vanilla extract

1 cup (80g) cocoa powder, sifted

¾ cup (90g) all-purpose flour, sifted

1 teaspoon baking powder

¼ cup (60ml) nondairy milk

1.   Preheat the oven to 350°F (176°C). Line an 8-inch (20cm) square baking pan with parchment paper.

2.   In a large bowl, whisk together the sugars, tahini, melted vegan butter, and melted chocolate until combined.

3.   Pour the egg replacers and vanilla extract into the bowl and whisk for 1 minute to add air to the mixture.

4.   Add the cocoa powder, flour, and baking powder and use a rubber spatula to mix. The mixture will be thick and more like a cookie dough than a batter. When it starts to clump together in little pieces, pour in the nondairy milk and continue to mix with the spatula until well combined, with no dry spots or loose cocoa powder left in the bowl.

5.   Use your hands to press the dough evenly into the prepared pan.

6.   Bake for 20 minutes, or until the brownies are still slightly moist and a bit fudgy in the center; a toothpick inserted in the middle will come out with fudgy crumbs attached.

7.   Let the brownies cool for 20 minutes before cutting with a sharp knife and serving. Store leftovers in a sealed container on the counter for up to 3 days.

iced sugar cookies

Yield: 16 cookies

Prep Time: 20 minutes, plus time to cool

Cook Time: 10 minutes

Sugar cookies are a staple that everyone should know how to make. They require only a few ingredients and are very easy to prepare. If you don't feel like being fancy, cut them into circles and decorate them with sprinkles, but this recipe is great for more elaborate cookies as well. Vegan sprinkles can be found online. Be sure to check the ingredients and avoid any product that contains confectioners' glaze, which is not vegan-friendly.

1 cup (224g) vegan butter, softened, plus more if needed

1 cup (192g) organic granulated sugar

1 egg replacer (see pages 11–12)

1 tablespoon vanilla extract

2¾ cups (330g) all-purpose flour, sifted

2 teaspoons baking powder

ICING

1 cup (120g) organic confectioners' sugar

2 tablespoons vegan sprinkles

1. Place one oven rack in the top third of the oven and a second rack in the bottom third. Preheat the oven to 400°F (204°C). Line 2 cookie sheets with parchment paper.

2. In a large bowl, mash the vegan butter and granulated sugar with the back of a fork until it resembles mashed potatoes. This can also be done with an electric hand mixer.

3. Pour in the egg replacer and vanilla extract and mix with a spoon to combine.

4. Add the flour and baking powder to the bowl. Mix with the spoon until the dough is crumbly. Knead the dough with your hands for 2 to 3 minutes, until it comes together. If it seems too dry and will not come together, add 1 tablespoon of softened vegan butter.

5. Form the dough into a large ball and then flatten it into a disc. Place the disc between 2 sheets of parchment paper and roll it out to ¼ inch (6mm) thick.

6. Use a 3½-inch (9cm) biscuit cutter, cookie cutter, or large cup to cut out 8 circles of dough. Place the dough circles on one of the prepared cookie sheets, spacing them 1½ inches (4cm) apart.

7. Cut as many additional dough circles as you can, then form the dough scraps into a ball again, flatten into a disc, and reroll to ¼ inch (6mm) thick. Cut additional dough circles, repeating this process until all of the dough has been used. You should get a total of 16 cookies. Place the other 8 dough circles on the second prepared cookie sheet.

8. Bake the cookies for 7 to 10 minutes, until the edges are slightly golden. Watch them carefully; the baking time may vary depending on your oven and pans.

9. Remove the cookies from the oven and allow to cool on the pans for 5 minutes, then transfer to a wire rack to cool for 1 hour before icing. Place the rack on top of one of the cookie sheets.

10. While the cookies are cooling, prepare the icing: Whisk the confectioners' sugar with 1 tablespoon of water in a medium-sized bowl that is large enough to fit the cookies. Keep adding ½ tablespoon of water at a time until the icing has the right consistency; it should be somewhat thick so it does not spread everywhere but thin enough to slowly drip off a spoon.

11. To ice the cookies, dip them into the icing, allow the excess to drip off, and place back on the wire rack. Cover the iced cookies with the sprinkles. Let the cookies sit for 5 to 10 minutes, or until the icing has hardened, before eating. Store in a sealed container on the counter for up to 3 days.

cream puffs

Yield: 10 cream puffs

Prep Time: 30 minutes, plus time to cool

Cook Time: 35 minutes

Homemade cream puffs were my great-grandma's specialty. I wanted to make a vegan version for years, but the main leavening agent in cream puffs is eggs. So how do we make a cream puff that still puffs without the eggs? It took a few rounds of testing and a lot of patience, but eventually these vegan cream puffs were born. They are filled with a light, creamy filling and sprinkled with a bit of confectioners' sugar for complete perfection. (Tip: Self-rising flour is the secret leavening agent here since eggs are not used. You can easily make self-rising flour by adding 1½ teaspoons of baking powder and ¼ teaspoon of salt to 1 cup [120g] of all-purpose flour.)

CREAM PUFF SHELLS

½ cup (112g) vegan butter

Pinch of turmeric powder

1 cup (120g) self-rising flour

½ teaspoon baking powder

4 egg replacers (see pages 11–12)

FILLING

1 cup (240ml) nondairy milk

1 (3-ounce/85g) box cook-and-serve vanilla pudding

3 tablespoons organic confectioners' sugar, plus more for topping

3 cups (100g) canned vegan whipped cream

Canned vegan whipped cream is preferable to Cocowhip in this recipe because it's lighter and airier, resulting in a lighter filling for the delicate pastry.

The filling calls for just half of the prepared pudding. You can store the remaining pudding in the refrigerator for up to 2 days and eat it separately.

Cream puffs are best enjoyed fresh, so it is best to fill only as many shells as you intend to eat right away. To store the baked and cooled shells, place them in a sealed container on the counter for up to 2 days (do not cut them). Store the filling in a separate container in the refrigerator for up to 2 days. When you are ready to eat a cream puff, you can cut the pastry shell and fill it.

1. Preheat the oven to 425°F (218°C). Line a rimmed baking sheet with parchment paper.

2. Prepare the shells: In a medium-sized saucepan, bring the vegan butter, turmeric, and 1 cup (240ml) of water to a rolling boil over high heat. Once boiling, reduce the heat to low and add the flour and baking powder. Mix with a wooden spoon until a ball of dough forms and a little film develops on the bottom of the pan.

3. Remove the pan from the heat. Pour in 1 egg replacer and mix with the wooden spoon. The dough will start to break apart, but it will come together again as you continue mixing. When the dough has come back together, repeat with the remaining 3 egg replacers.

4. Scoop 2 heaping tablespoons of the dough into your hands and roll into a rough ball. Place on the lined baking sheet. Repeat with the remaining dough, making a total of 10 balls.

5. Bake for 25 minutes, or until golden brown. Do not open the oven door while the shells bake.

6. Meanwhile, prepare the pudding: Pour the nondairy milk into a medium-sized saucepan and stir in the pudding mix. Bring to a boil over medium heat, stirring occasionally. When it reaches a boil, remove from the heat. Refrigerate the pudding for 1 hour.

7. Remove the shells from the oven and let cool completely on the pan, about 2 hours.

8. When the shells are completely cool, use a serrated knife to cut the top third off of each shell and remove the dough from the inside.

9. Prepare the filling: In a medium-sized bowl, mix together half of the prepared pudding and the confectioners' sugar. Then carefully fold in the whipped cream until just combined so the filling does not lose its airiness.

10. Scoop 1 tablespoon of the filling into each shell. If you have leftover filling, divide it equally among the cream puffs. Place the tops of the shells back on, then sift confectioners' sugar over the tops of the cream puffs.

black and white cookies

Yield: 8 cookies

Prep Time: 25 minutes, plus time to cool

Cook Time: 16 minutes

A New York deli classic, black and white cookies have been around for a long time. They have a very specific texture, more cakelike than cookie. They are iced with half vanilla and half chocolate icing, and if you ask anybody who grew up eating these cookies, they will tell you that they definitely have a favorite side to eat! Mine is chocolate all the way.

½ cup (120ml) nondairy milk

1 teaspoon apple cider vinegar

⅓ cup (75g) vegan butter, softened

½ cup (96g) organic granulated sugar

1 egg replacer (see pages 11–12)

1 teaspoon vanilla extract

1½ cups (180g) all-purpose flour

1 teaspoon baking powder

¼ teaspoon baking soda

ICING

2 cups (240g) organic confectioners' sugar

1 tablespoon light corn syrup

2 tablespoons cocoa powder

Store leftover cookies in a sealed container on the counter. They are best eaten within 1 to 2 days.

1. Preheat the oven to 350°F (176°C). Line a cookie sheet with parchment paper.

2. In a liquid measuring cup or small glass bowl, mix together the nondairy milk and vinegar. Set aside to curdle for 10 minutes.

3. In a medium-sized bowl, use an electric mixer to cream the vegan butter and granulated sugar until light and fluffy.

4. Add the nondairy milk mixture, egg replacer, and vanilla extract to the bowl with the creamed butter and sugar. Mix until combined.

5. In a separate bowl, whisk together the flour, baking powder, and baking soda. Add the dry ingredients to the wet ingredients and use a rubber spatula to mix until everything is well combined and a thick dough has formed.

6. Drop 3-tablespoon portions of the dough onto the prepared cookie sheet, leaving 3 inches (8cm) of space between them. You should have a total of 8 cookies. Using the back of a spoon, form each portion of dough into a 3-inch (8cm) circle.

7. Bake the cookies for 14 to 16 minutes, until puffed and lightly golden on the edges. Let cool for at least 1 hour before icing.

8. Prepare the icing: In a medium-sized bowl, mix together the confectioners' sugar, corn syrup, and 2 tablespoons of water. The icing should be easy to spread but not runny. If necessary, add 1 to 2 teaspoons more water.

9. Flip the cookies over so the flat bottoms are faceup. Using an offset spatula, carefully spread the vanilla icing over half of each cookie. When all of the halves have been iced, stir the cocoa powder into the icing to make chocolate icing. Add 1 to 2 teaspoons of water if needed to make it spreadable. Ice the other halves of the cookies with the chocolate icing. Let the icing set for 10 minutes before eating the cookies.

mini salted caramel "cheesecake"

Yield: 4 to 6 servings

Prep Time: 20 minutes, plus time to chill caramel sauce and cake

Cook Time: 1 hour 20 minutes

Good things really do come in small packages. The flavor and texture of this mini vegan cheesecake are sure to wow you. The chocolate cookie crust paired with a light, creamy filling and topped with a decadent sweet and salty homemade caramel sauce is just too good to beat. It may take all of your willpower to wait for the cake to chill, though!

SALTED CARAMEL SAUCE
(Makes ¾ to 1 cup/225g to 300g)

1 cup (192g) organic granulated sugar

½ cup (120ml) nondairy milk

¼ cup (56g) vegan butter

¼ teaspoon salt, or more to taste

CRUST

25 vegan chocolate sandwich cookies

1 tablespoon melted vegan butter, if needed

FILLING

1 (16-ounce/454g) block silken tofu

1 scant cup (7 ounces/200g) vegan cream cheese

⅔ cup (128g) organic granulated sugar

¼ cup (75g) salted caramel sauce (from above)

1 teaspoon vanilla extract

¼ teaspoon coarse sea salt, for sprinkling

SPECIAL EQUIPMENT:
6 by 3-inch (15 by 8cm) springform pan

High-powered blender

1. Prepare the caramel sauce: In a 2-quart saucepan, slowly dissolve the sugar in ½ cup (120ml) of water over medium-low heat, stirring. When the mixture starts to boil gently, raise the heat to high and boil *without stirring* for 6 to 7 minutes, until it is a medium amber color. Watch it carefully so it doesn't burn. (If it's burning, you will notice the color getting very dark brown; if that happens, remove the pan from the heat immediately. If the caramel is only slightly burnt, you may be able to salvage it; if it is very burnt, however, it's best to start over.)

2. Remove the pan from the heat and slowly pour in the nondairy milk, then stir with a wooden spoon. Add the vegan butter and salt and mix until uniform. Carefully taste the sauce (it will be warm) and add more salt if you like. Transfer the sauce to a glass jar and refrigerate for at least 4 hours or overnight to thicken.

3. After the caramel sauce has thickened, preheat the oven to 350°F (176°C). Generously grease a 6 by 3-inch (15 by 8cm) springform pan with cooking spray.

4. Prepare the crust: Place the cookies in a high-powered blender or food processor and pulse until completely broken down into fine crumbs. Using your hands, press the cookie crumbs evenly into the greased springform pan; try not to let it be too thin anywhere. Start by pressing it into the base and then work it up the sides, stopping about ½ inch (13mm) from the rim of the pan. If the crust is too dry, pour in 1 tablespoon of melted vegan butter to help it stick.

5. Prepare the filling: Place all of the filling ingredients in a high-powered blender and blend until very smooth. Pour the filling into the crust. It should almost reach the top of the crust but not exceed it. If you end up with leftover filling, you can store it in the fridge for up to 3 days and use it as a dip for fruit or cookies.

If your caramel sauce does not thicken after chilling, put it back in the saucepan and place it over medium heat. Cook until it has reduced by half, then place it in the refrigerator to chill for another 2 hours. Leftover caramel sauce can be stored in the refrigerator for up to 6 days.

6. Bake the cheesecake for 70 minutes, until it is slightly jiggly in the center and golden on top but set on the edges.

7. Turn off the oven, open the oven door, and let the cake rest for 20 minutes. Then remove it from the oven and let it cool on the counter for 20 minutes. Finally, place it in the refrigerator for at least 5 hours or overnight to fully chill.

8. When ready to serve, drizzle the cake with the desired amount of caramel sauce and sprinkle with the coarse salt. Cut into slices and serve.

rainbow cookies

Yield: 16 (2-inch/5cm) cookies

Prep Time: 25 minutes, plus time to chill layers

Cook Time: 15 minutes

Rainbow cookies are a special treat and are usually eaten around the holidays. They aren't difficult to make, but they do require a bit of time to prepare because the layers have to be weighted down to compress them. However, I promise that these cookies are incredible. The traditional colors are the green, white, and red of the Italian flag, but you can use any colors you like; just be sure to buy vegan-friendly food dyes. There are plenty of options available online.

Liquid from 1 (15½-ounce/439g) can chickpeas

8 ounces (225g) almond paste

1 cup (192g) organic granulated sugar

1¼ cups (280g) vegan butter, softened

3 egg replacers (see pages 11–12)

1 teaspoon vanilla extract

2 cups (240g) all-purpose flour

Green vegan food dye, or other color of choice

Red vegan food dye, or other color of choice

½ cup (152g) apricot preserves, divided

½ cup (120g) vegan dark chocolate chips (about 70% cacao)

2 tablespoons nondairy milk

1. Place one oven rack in the top third of the oven and a second rack in the bottom third. Preheat the oven to 350°F (176°C). Line three 8-inch (20cm) square baking pans with parchment paper. (*Note:* If you have only one or two pans, you can bake the layers in batches.)

2. Pour the chickpea brine into a large bowl. Use an electric mixer to whip the brine on high speed for 4 to 5 minutes, until stiff peaks form. This is aquafaba.

3. Using your hands, begin to crumble the almond paste into a second large bowl, then use an electric mixer to break up the paste further for 1 minute. Add the sugar and mix until very small crumbles form, almost resembling sand.

4. Add the vegan butter and whip on high speed until fluffy and pale, about 3 minutes. Pour in the egg replacers and vanilla extract and gently mix on low speed for 30 seconds just until incorporated.

5. With the mixer on low speed, slowly add the flour. After all of the flour is added, increase the speed to medium and continue to mix the batter until combined. It will be thick.

6. Add about a third of the aquafaba and mix with a spatula to loosen the batter slightly. Then add the rest of the aquafaba and gently fold it in so the batter doesn't lose its airiness.

7. Divide the batter into thirds. Dye one batch green and one batch red, leaving the third batch as is. For a medium color intensity, use 15 drops of green and 10 drops of red.

8. Scoop the batter into the prepared baking pans and use an offset spatula to spread it out and make the tops flat and even. The layers will be thin but will puff up slightly as they bake. Bake for 15 minutes, until slightly golden and dry on top. Allow the layers to cool in the pans for 1 hour. Before assembling, remove the white and green layers from their pans and peel off the parchment paper; leave the red layer in its pan.

9. To assemble, use the offset spatula to very thinly spread half of the apricot preserves over the red layer. Place the white layer on top. Spread the rest of the preserves over the white layer, then set the green layer on top. If a layer cracks or breaks, it's okay; just put it back together. Place a clean 8-inch (20cm) square baking pan on top of the green layer, then weight it down with heavy cans of tomato sauce or beans. This helps compress and adhere the layers. Place the pan in the refrigerator to chill for at least 4 hours or overnight.

10. After the cookie layers have chilled, melt the chocolate chips with the nondairy milk in the microwave in 30-second intervals, stirring after each interval. The mixture should be thick, not liquidy, but easy to spread.

11. Remove the pan from the refrigerator, remove the top pan, and carefully unpan the layered dessert. Remove the parchment paper from the bottom red layer and place the stack on a rimmed baking sheet. Spread the chocolate mixture evenly over the layers; if you like, you can use a fork to make a design in the chocolate, as shown. Place the baking sheet in the refrigerator to chill for 1 hour, or until the chocolate is set.

12. Using a serrated knife, cut the chocolate-topped layers into 16 squares, or, if you prefer smaller pieces, cut them to your liking. You can also trim the sides to make perfect squares. These cookies are best stored in the refrigerator; they'll keep for up to 5 days.

Some brands of almond paste are sold in 7-ounce (200g) tubes; if this is the only size you can find, it is okay to use that amount for this recipe.

strawberry shortcake

Yield: 6 to 8 servings

Prep Time: 20 minutes, plus time for cakes to cool

Cook Time: 20 minutes

Need a dessert that looks impressive but is easy to make? Strawberry shortcake is the answer. Layers of light, almost biscuitlike cake topped with cream and strawberries make this a delicious and beautiful dessert. Be sure to store any leftovers in the fridge.

½ cup plus 2 tablespoons (120g) organic granulated sugar, divided

5 tablespoons (70g) vegan butter, softened

1 cup (240ml) nondairy milk

2 tablespoons vegan sour cream

1 egg replacer (see pages 11–12)

1 teaspoon vanilla extract

2 cups (240g) all-purpose flour

1 tablespoon baking powder

1 teaspoon baking soda

1 (9-ounce/225g) container Cocowhip coconut whipped topping

¼ cup (2 ounces/55g) vegan cream cheese

1 quart (500g) strawberries, sliced

1. Preheat the oven to 400°F (204°C). Grease the sides of two 8-inch (20cm) round cake pans and line the bottoms with parchment paper.

2. Using an electric mixer, cream ½ cup (96g) of the sugar and the vegan butter in a bowl until light and fluffy. Mix in the nondairy milk, vegan sour cream, egg replacer, and vanilla extract just until incorporated.

3. In a second larger bowl, whisk together the flour, baking powder, and baking soda.

4. Pour the wet ingredients into the dry ingredients and mix with a spatula to combine. The batter will be fluffy and sticky; it is not like regular cake batter. Just mix until it comes together.

5. Divide the batter evenly between the prepared pans and use an offset spatula or a spoon to smooth the tops. Bake for 20 minutes, or until the cakes are golden brown and a toothpick inserted in the center of a cake comes out clean.

6. Meanwhile, with an electric mixer or in a blender, mix the coconut whipped topping and vegan cream cheese until combined. Refrigerate until ready to use.

7. In a separate bowl, mix the strawberries with the remaining 2 tablespoons of sugar. Place this bowl in the refrigerator as well.

8. When the cakes are done, remove them from the pans, peel off the parchment paper, and place on a wire rack to cool for at least 1 hour.

9. To assemble, spread half of the coconut whipped topping mixture on one of the cakes. Top with half of the strawberries, keeping them as flat and even as possible so the next layer is not lopsided. Repeat with the remaining cake, coconut whipped topping mixture, and strawberries.

10. Place the dessert in the refrigerator to chill until ready to serve. Leftovers will keep in the fridge for up to 2 days.

zeppole

Yield: 30 zeppole (6 to 10 servings)

Prep Time: 10 minutes, plus time for dough to rise

Cook Time: 20 minutes

Nothing says summer and street food to me more than zeppole. When I was little, we used to go to the fairs in town, and they always sold zeppole. You ate them hot, fresh out of the deep fryer in a greasy paper bag, and nothing tasted better. Luckily, zeppole are easy to make at home. They are just little bits of fried dough topped with confectioners' sugar. If you don't feel like making homemade dough, store-bought pizza dough works great, or you might even be able to buy dough from your local pizzeria.

1 (¼-ounce/7g) packet active dry yeast

1 tablespoon organic granulated sugar

2 cups (240g) all-purpose flour

¼ teaspoon salt

1 tablespoon olive oil, plus more for the bowl

2 cups (475ml) canola or vegetable oil, for frying

¼ cup (30g) organic confectioners' sugar, for topping

Zeppole are best enjoyed hot and fresh. However, if you have leftovers, you can store them in a rolled-up paper bag. To reheat, place in a preheated 350°F (176°C) oven for 5 minutes, or until warm. You can then sprinkle them with extra confectioners' sugar.

1. Prepare the dough: Pour the yeast into ½ cup (120ml) of warm water that is between 100°F and 110°F (37°C and 43°C). Add the granulated sugar and set aside to proof for 10 minutes, until foamy.

2. In a large bowl, whisk together the flour and salt. When the yeast has proofed, add it to the bowl along with the 1 tablespoon of olive oil. Mix with a spoon until the dough is shaggy. Using your hands, knead the dough for 5 to 10 minutes, until a smooth ball forms.

3. Place the dough in a well-oiled bowl, cover with a clean kitchen towel, and allow to rise for 1 hour, or until doubled in size.

4. After the dough has risen and you are ready to fry the zeppole, heat the canola oil to 350°F (176°C) in a 2-quart saucepan over medium heat.

5. To form the zeppole, rip off about 1 tablespoon of the dough and roll it into a 1-inch (2.5cm) ball. Repeat until all of the dough has been used; you should get about 30 zeppole.

6. When the oil has come to temperature, place 10 zeppole in the oil and fry for 5 to 7 minutes, still over medium heat. Use a spoon to move them around and ensure that all sides are getting fried. The zeppole will puff up as they fry. When they are golden, remove from the oil with a slotted spoon and place on a dish lined with a paper towel. Repeat with the remaining zeppole.

7. Place the zeppole in a paper bag with the confectioners' sugar and shake to coat. Enjoy warm straight from the bag.

affogato

Yield: 1 serving

Prep Time: 10 minutes
(not including time to brew
espresso)

The Italian verb affogare *means "to drown" in English. For this dessert, you "drown" ice cream in espresso. In Italy, affogato is typically served with vanilla gelato, but vegan ice cream is just as delicious, and you can get creative by using any flavor you like. Hot espresso is poured right over the ice cream, which melts, of course. (See the note below for an espresso substitution.) This dessert is so pretty, too.*

2 scoops (⅔ cup/140g) vegan
vanilla ice cream

1 double shot (2 ounces/60ml)
espresso

Place the vegan ice cream in a small heatproof glass or cup.
Pour the hot espresso over the ice cream. Enjoy immediately.

*If you don't have an espresso
machine, you can use instant
espresso powder or substitute
¼ cup (60ml) of strong brewed
coffee. You can also add toppings
such as canned vegan whipped
cream, vegan chocolate shavings,
or ground cinnamon.*

cinnamon apple bundt cake

Yield: 8 servings

Prep Time: 20 minutes, plus time to cool

Cook Time: 1 hour

I love Bundt cakes because you get a beautiful design without any hard work. This cake is full of cinnamon and apples and is topped with a simple sweet glaze; it's perfect for cold fall and winter nights. Enjoy it with a warm cup of coffee or tea for maximum coziness.

3 cups (360g) all-purpose flour

1 tablespoon ground cinnamon, plus more for garnish if desired

2 teaspoons baking powder

¾ cup (145g) organic granulated sugar

¾ cup (145g) organic dark brown sugar

½ cup (120ml) nondairy milk

½ cup (112g) vegan butter, melted

¼ cup (60g) vegan sour cream

2 egg replacers (see pages 11–12)

1 teaspoon vanilla extract

2½ cups (270g) chopped Granny Smith apples (about 3 apples)

GLAZE

1¼ cups (150g) confectioners' sugar

1. Preheat the oven to 350°F (176°C). Grease a 12-cup (3L) Bundt pan with a flour-based baking spray.

2. In a large bowl, whisk together the flour, cinnamon, and baking powder.

3. Place the sugars, nondairy milk, melted vegan butter, vegan sour cream, egg replacers, and vanilla extract in a separate large bowl. Use an electric mixer to mix on medium-low speed for 30 to 40 seconds, until well combined.

4. Gradually add the dry ingredients to the bowl with the wet ingredients and continue to mix on medium-low speed for 30 to 40 seconds, until well combined and smooth, scraping down the sides of the bowl as necessary. Do not overmix. The batter will be very thick.

5. Use a rubber spatula to fold in the chopped apples. Pour the batter into the greased Bundt pan and spread evenly with the spatula.

6. Bake for 50 to 60 minutes, until a toothpick inserted in the center of the cake comes out clean. Let cool in the pan for 15 minutes, then invert the pan over a plate to release the cake. Let cool for at least 2 hours or overnight (see note, opposite) before glazing.

7. Prepare the glaze: In a medium-sized bowl, mix the confectioners' sugar with 1 tablespoon of water. The glaze should be thin enough to drizzle from a spoon but thick enough that it appears white rather than transparent.

8. To glaze the cake, set a wire rack inside a rimmed baking sheet lined with parchment paper for easy cleanup. Place the cake on the rack and pour the glaze over it, allowing the excess to drip off. Sprinkle with cinnamon, if desired. Allow the glaze to set for at least 5 minutes before slicing and serving the cake. Store leftover glazed cake on a plate, covered with aluminum foil, on the counter for up to 2 days.

I find flour-based baking spray to be a necessity when making a Bundt cake, as it makes the cake easier to remove from the pan. Without it, the batter is much more likely to stick to the nooks and crannies in the fluted pan. I prefer the spray from the brand PAM, but any baking spray that contains flour is fine.

You can make this cake a day ahead and glaze it the next day if you like. Store the cooled, unglazed cake on a plate, loosely covered with aluminum foil, on the counter.

perfect chocolate chip cookies

Yield: 12 cookies
Prep Time: 10 minutes
Cook Time: 9 minutes

Everyone needs to know how to make chocolate chip cookies. They are a classic and, when baked correctly, I would have to say they're the best cookie. This vegan version is gooey, chewy, and soft, with the perfect amount of chocolate chips. These cookies require just a few simple ingredients, and you do not need to chill the dough prior to baking.

½ cup (112g) vegan butter, softened

½ cup (96g) organic dark brown sugar

¼ cup (48g) organic granulated sugar

1 egg replacer (see pages 11–12)

1 teaspoon vanilla extract

1¼ cups (150g) all-purpose flour

1 teaspoon baking powder

⅓ heaping cup (95g) vegan semisweet chocolate chips, divided

1. Preheat the oven to 375°F (196°C). Line a cookie sheet with parchment paper.

2. In a large bowl, use an electric mixer to cream the vegan butter and sugars for about 3 minutes, until light and fluffy. Pour in the egg replacer and vanilla extract and mix until well incorporated.

3. Sift the flour and baking powder into the bowl. Mix with a wooden spoon until a thick, smooth dough has formed. Fold in the chocolate chips.

4. Scoop up 1 heaping tablespoon of the dough and use your hands to roll it into a ball. Place the ball on the parchment-lined cookie sheet. Repeat with the remaining dough, making a total of 12 cookies. Space the cookie dough balls about 1½ inches (4cm) apart.

5. Bake for 9 minutes, or until the cookies are very lightly golden around the edges but still pale in color. They will be very soft when they come out of the oven. Leave them on the cookie sheet for 10 minutes to continue cooking slightly and firm up.

6. Enjoy warm or let cool before serving or storing. Store leftovers in a sealed container on the counter for up to 3 days.

6.

basics

This short chapter features essential recipes that you will use to make other recipes in this cookbook. All of them are great components to know how to make, and all of them can be prepped in advance to get meals on the table even quicker and more easily.

tempeh bacon crumbles

Yield: about ⅔ cup (150g) (11 servings)

Prep Time: 5 minutes, plus time to marinate

Cook Time: 25 minutes

Tempeh bacon is one of my favorite bacon replacers. Due to tempeh's naturally meaty texture and ability to soak up a marinade, it really is the perfect substitute. It gets crispy when pan-fried and makes a tasty topping for Cobb Salad (page 134) or Broccoli and Cheddar Twice-Baked Potatoes (page 106).

4 ounces (115g) tempeh

1½ tablespoons low-sodium soy sauce

1½ teaspoons olive oil

2 teaspoons organic dark brown sugar

½ teaspoon garlic powder

½ teaspoon onion powder

½ teaspoon smoked paprika

¼ teaspoon ground black pepper

Pinch of cayenne pepper

1. Using your hands, crumble the tempeh into small pieces directly into a medium-sized nonstick frying pan. Pour ¼ cup (60ml) of water over the tempeh. Cover with a lid and steam over medium-high heat for 15 minutes, or until all of the water has been absorbed.

2. Meanwhile, make the marinade: In a container, mix together the soy sauce, oil, brown sugar, seasonings, and 2 tablespoons of water.

3. Add the steamed tempeh to the container with the marinade. Seal the lid and shake to coat the tempeh. Place in the refrigerator to marinate for at least 1 hour or up to 12 hours.

4. Just before using, remove the tempeh from the marinade and put it in a small nonstick frying pan; discard the marinade. Sauté over medium heat, stirring occasionally with a rubber spatula, for 10 minutes, or until the tempeh is crispy.

5. Use immediately or store in the refrigerator for up to 4 days.

vegan buttermilk ranch dressing

Yield: 1 cup (245g) (8 servings)

Prep Time: 5 minutes, plus time to chill

I think we can all agree that ranch dressing is a favorite. While there are many good vegan ranch dressings available to buy, making your own is easy, and the result is always delicious. This dressing is the star of my Cobb Salad (page 134) and also works great as a dip for Popcorn Chick'n (page 62) or Onion Rings (page 72). Keep a fresh batch of this classic dressing in your fridge for when a ranch craving strikes.

½ cup (120ml) nondairy milk

1 teaspoon apple cider vinegar

½ cup (120g) vegan sour cream

1 teaspoon maple syrup

1 teaspoon vegetable oil

1½ teaspoons garlic powder

1½ teaspoons onion powder

¼ teaspoon dried parsley

¼ teaspoon salt

¼ teaspoon ground black pepper

1. Pour the nondairy milk and vinegar into a medium-sized glass bowl. Set aside for 2 to 3 minutes, until the milk starts to curdle (this is the "buttermilk").

2. Add the vegan sour cream, maple syrup, and oil to the bowl and whisk until smooth, then add the seasonings and mix well to incorporate. Place in the refrigerator to chill for at least 1 hour or overnight before using. The dressing will keep in the refrigerator for up to 3 days.

tofu ricotta

Yield: 2¼ cups (500g)
(4 servings)

Prep Time: 5 minutes

Believe it or not, tofu works very well as a creamy base for vegan ricotta. This nondairy cheese is good enough to fool even non-vegans—trust me! It works great in my Meaty Vegan Lasagna (page 110), Spinach and Tofu Ricotta–Stuffed Shells (page 128), Homemade Manicotti (page 124), and so many other dishes.

1 (14-ounce/397g) block firm tofu, crumbled

¼ cup (60ml) nondairy milk

1 tablespoon lemon juice

1 tablespoon nutritional yeast

½ teaspoon salt, or to taste

1. Place all of the ingredients in a blender or food processor. Blend on medium speed for 1 minute, until the mixture is mostly smooth with very small pieces of tofu remaining.

2. Use immediately or store in the refrigerator for up to 4 days.

tomato sauce

Yield: 3 cups (775g)
(6 servings)
Prep Time: 5 minutes
Cook Time: 25 minutes

There are many great store-bought tomato sauces out there, but nothing compares to a homemade sauce. Tomato sauce is very easy to make and requires only a few ingredients. A good sauce doesn't need to be overly seasoned—it all starts with using good-quality canned tomatoes. San Marzano tomatoes tend to be sweeter and a little less acidic than other varieties, so I definitely recommend using them. If you can't find them, though, don't worry; you can use San Marzano–style tomatoes or plum tomatoes instead.

1 tablespoon olive oil

¼ onion, preferably Vidalia (about 2 ounces/55g), chopped

2 cloves garlic, minced

1 (28-ounce/794g) can San Marzano tomatoes, undrained

1 tablespoon organic granulated sugar, or more as needed

¼ teaspoon salt

Pinch of red pepper flakes

1. Heat the oil in a large sauté pan over medium heat for 1 minute. Add the onion and garlic and sauté for 5 minutes, until the onion is translucent and the garlic is fragrant. Do not let the garlic burn; if it is cooking too fast, lower the heat.

2. Meanwhile, pour the tomatoes and their juice into a blender and pulse on medium speed for 30 seconds to 1 minute, just enough to break down the tomatoes but leaving a little bit of texture. Fill the tomato can one-quarter of the way full with water and slosh it around to dislodge any bits of tomatoes or juice from the bottom of the can.

3. Pour the pureed tomatoes along with the water from the can into the pan with the onion and garlic and stir with a wooden spoon. Sprinkle with the sugar, salt, and red pepper flakes and stir to combine.

4. Reduce the heat to medium-low and simmer the sauce uncovered, stirring occasionally, for 20 minutes. It should be lightly bubbling. The sauce will thicken and should taste slightly sweet. If it tastes too acidic, add another 1 to 2 teaspoons of sugar.

5. Use immediately, store in the refrigerator for up to 3 days, or freeze for up to 1 month and thaw before use.

homemade vegan mozzarella

Yield: 1½ cups (400g)
(3 servings)

Prep Time: 5 minutes

Cook Time: 35 minutes

I am extremely proud of this recipe. Vegan cheese is not always easy to find, and recipes for homemade vegan cheese sometimes call for obscure ingredients. This allergy-friendly version, however, uses just five readily accessible ingredients and is simple to make. Note that this recipe makes what I would call a vegan cheese sauce; it cannot be formed into a solid shape and cannot be shredded or cubed. When a recipe in this book, such as Meaty Vegan Lasagna (page 110) or Mozzarella in Carrozza (page 60), calls for Homemade Vegan Mozzarella, it refers to this recipe; if it calls for vegan mozzarella shreds or cubes, I intend for you to use the type sold in stores. Also note that a high-powered blender is important for this recipe, as it will ensure that the vegan mozzarella is smooth.

---

1 small or ½ large head cauliflower (about 10½ ounces/300g), cored and cut into florets

½ cup (120ml) nondairy milk

¼ cup (30g) tapioca starch

1 tablespoon nutritional yeast

½ teaspoon salt, or more to taste

SPECIAL EQUIPMENT:
High-powered blender

1. Put the cauliflower florets in a medium-sized saucepan, add enough water to cover, and bring to a boil over high heat. Continue to boil for 30 minutes, or until the cauliflower is extremely soft when pierced with a fork.

2. Drain the cauliflower and place it in a high-powered blender with the remaining ingredients. Blend on high speed until smooth. It will be a very thin liquid; it will thicken once it is cooked.

3. Pour the mixture into the saucepan you used to cook the cauliflower and cook over medium heat, stirring often with a rubber spatula, for 5 to 7 minutes. As it heats up, the tapioca starch will be activated and the sauce will thicken. The sauce is done when it turns gooey, like molten cheese.

4. Use immediately or store in the refrigerator for up to 2 days.

The longer this cheese sits, the stronger the cauliflower smell and taste become, so it really is best used immediately after making it. It can also be frozen and then thawed overnight before use. When using this vegan mozzarella, I find it easiest to portion out the amount needed in a dry measuring cup. It spreads easily with a rubber spatula.

perfect white rice

Yield: 4 cups (700g)
(4 servings)

Prep Time: 1 minute

Cook Time: 25 minutes

Fluffy white rice is something everyone should know how to make. The key to perfect rice is to cook it over very low heat; this allows it to steam. You can serve this rice as a side with dishes like the Sesame Tofu Bowl (page 90) or use it in any recipe that calls for cooked white rice, such as Arancini (page 48).

1⅓ cups (240g) long-grain white rice

Pinch of salt

1. Bring the rice, salt, and 2⅔ cups (630ml) of water to a boil in a medium-sized saucepan over high heat. When it reaches a boil, reduce the heat to low. Cover and gently simmer for 20 minutes, or until the rice has absorbed all of the water. Fluff with a fork before serving.

2. Use immediately or store in the refrigerator for up to 2 days.

To store, transfer the cooked rice to a storage container and allow it to cool, then immediately refrigerate it. Keep cooked rice for no longer than 2 days, and do not reheat it multiple times.

acknowledgments

I thank my amazing parents, Phil and Alyssa, for all of their support and love. They have always believed in me in whatever I have done, and I wouldn't be half the person I am today without them.

To my younger sister and brother, Gabriella and Anthony, who are always proud of me, tasting my recipes and supporting me.

Thank you to my grandma Zucchi, who has always encouraged and helped me during the creative process.

Thank you to my grandpa for his appreciation and support of all that I do.

Thank you to my doggies, Bella and Roxy, who keep me company all day long and make me laugh when they try to sneak a little taste of what I'm cooking.

Thank you to my friends, who have been here for me since day one and believed in everything I was doing, even when I didn't.

Finally, thank you to my followers; without you all, I wouldn't be where I am, and something like this cookbook never would have been possible. I am so grateful for everyone who has been there for me; the support means more than anyone will ever know.

recipe index

1. *breakfast comfort*

48 Arancini

50 Spinach Fritters

52 Betty Grandma's Meatballs

54 Greek Nachos

56 Vegetable Spring Rolls

58 Hummus-Stuffed Falafel

60 Mozzarella in Carrozza

62 Popcorn Chick'n

64 Vegan Cheddar and Potato Pierogi

66 Southern "Buttermilk" Biscuits

68 Spinach and Artichoke Dip

70 Sweet Gochujang Tempeh Bao

72 Onion Rings

74 Vegetable Dumplings

76 French Onion Soup

78 Scallion Pancakes

80 Poutine

3. comfort bowls

84 Creamy Balsamic Roasted Cauliflower Bowl

86 Peanut Tempeh Bowl

88 Fried Tofu with Garlic Mashed Potatoes Bowl

90 Sesame Tofu Bowl

92 Nourish Bowl

94 Pad Thai Bowl

96 "Beef" Bulgogi Bowl

98 Thai Red Curry Roasted Cauliflower Bowl

100 Southwestern Polenta Bowl

102 Bang Bang Tofu Bowl

4. mains

106 Broccoli and Cheddar Twice-Baked Potatoes

108 Buffalo Chick'n Sandwiches

110 Meaty Vegan Lasagna

112 Sheet Pan Tofu Cutlets with Roasted Vegetables

114 Deep Dish Pizza

116 Escarole and Beans

118 Meaty Vegan Burgers

120 Yellow Split Pea Cannellini Bean Stew

122 Lentil Sloppy Joes

124 Homemade Manicotti

126 Chick'n Marsala

128 Spinach and Tofu Ricotta–Stuffed Shells

130 White Chick'n Chili

132 Vegan Mac and Cheese

134 Cobb Salad with Vegan Buttermilk Ranch Dressing

136 Creamy "Beefy" Shells

138 Homemade Gnocchi with Vegan Butter Thyme Sauce

140 Kale, White Bean, and Vegan Sausage Skillet

142 Vegan Philly "Cheese Steak"

144 Creamy Lemon Pasta

146 Taco Casserole

148 Chick'n and Dumplings

150 Minestrone

5. desserts

154 Arroz con Leche

156 Baked Apple Empanadas

158 Vanilla Cupcakes with Vanilla Buttercream

160 Banana Pudding Pie

162 Fudgy Brownies

164 Iced Sugar Cookies

166 Cream Puffs

168 Black and White Cookies

170 Mini Salted Caramel "Cheesecake"

172 Rainbow Cookies

174 Strawberry Shortcake

176 Zeppole

178 Affogato

180 Cinnamon Apple Bundt Cake

182 Perfect Chocolate Chip Cookies

general index

about the author

Francesca Bonadonna is the force behind Plantifully Based, the wildly popular destination site for vegan inspiration, ideas, and recipes. At the age of twenty-three, while pursuing her study of opera, she experimented with a thirty-day vegan trial. Once she discovered the extraordinary benefits, her experiment became her lifestyle. In 2016, she decided to bring her passion to the world. Combining her love of food and her ability to make strong connections with people, she began to build her presence online.

Today, Francesca lives in New York, where she brings daily food joy through her amazing recipe creations, beautiful photography, and creative food styling. She delivers plant-based, vegan-friendly comforting flavors and textures that are healthy and approachable.

For more on Francesca and her journey, visit https://plantifullybasedblog.com, follow her Instagram, @plantifullybased, and visit her YouTube channel.